AF553808

INFANT HEALTH

A SOCIO-DEMOGRAPHIC ANALYSIS

INFANT HEALTH

A SOCIO-DEMOGRAPHIC ANALYSIS

By

Dr. B. Prabhakara Reddy

&

Dr. T. Lakshmamma

Dept. of Population Studies

Sri Venkateswara University

Tirupati–517 502 (A.P.)

India

DISCOVERY PUBLISHING HOUSE PVT. LTD.

NEW DELHI-110 002

First Published-2008

ISBN 978-81-8356-329-1

Published by:

DISCOVERY PUBLISHING HOUSE PVT. LTD.

4831/24, Ansari Road, Prahlad Street,
Darya Ganj, New Delhi-110002 (India)
Phone: 23279245 • Fax: 91-11-23253475
E-mail: dphbooks@rediffmail.com
dphtemp@indiatimes.com
Website: www.discoverypublishinghouse.com

Printed at:
Arora Enterprises
Laxmi Nagar, Delhi-110 092

Dedicatged
to my beloved father
Late SRI BUDIGI CHENDRASEKHARA REDDY
former V.M. of Irala

Preface

Children are the most vulnerable group of the population. If better infant health is provided child welfare programmes will succeed. Infant mortality rate is the highest in Africa and South Asia. The causes of poor health of infants are related to health and nutritional status of expectant and nursing mother.

Infant mortality rate in India has declared considerably especially after independence. But still the rate is alarmingly high compared to even some of the developing countries with wide regional variations within in the country. A number of studies have been conducted in the area of infant health and infant mortality.

The present book discussed on nutritional anthropometrical measurement of infant health status in a very backward area of South India, Kuppam Mandal of Chittoor district. There is a necessity of longitudinal study to study, the situation of health in their backward area to through light on this problem. The information presented in this book in based in original primary data collected by a team of investigators by door-to-door survey.

This work is invaluable for students of social sciences, particularly those interested in population studies and Health, Management sciences, and also for administrators those involved in the implementation of socio-economic development programmes. This volume is a significant contribution to the existing body of knowledge in the growing field of population sciences.

Authors

Acknowledgement

This study is the outcome of deep understanding, unstinted support, cooperation and discussion of two people. I am very deeply indebted to them. Particularly, I wish to express my gratitude and sincere thanks to Professor P.B. Jorapur. In spite of his retirement as professor from the Department of Population Studies, S.V. University, Tirupati, he provided invaluable guidance. Secondly, I wish to express my deep sense of gratitude to Dr. T. Lakshmamma, Research Associate, Department of Population Studies, S.V. University, Tirupati, for her continuous assistance during the period of this study.

I am also take this opportunity to express my sincere thanks to Kumari Madhavi, Smt. Geeta Gowri, and Smt. Dhanalakshmi former post-graduate students of Population Studies, S.V. University, Tirupati, for collecting the data.

My thanks are due to Sri Balakrishna, School of Humanities and Extension Studies, S.V. University, Tirupati, for his efficient handling of first draft of the typing work. I wish to thank Raju, Computer Job Typing, Tirupati, for word processing and for the draft of typing.

Contents

1

INTRODUCTION AND REVIEW OF LITERATURE

Introduction

Children are the most vulnerable group of the population. According to 1981 Census of India, the children of the age group 0-14 constitute 39.6 per cent of the total population and infants (under one year of age) constitute 2.5 per cent of the total population in India (Registrar General of India, 1983: 8). Large number of babies are born in India and many of them die also. In the year 1989 about 24.84 million babies were born and before they were one year old 2.26 million infants died (calculated according to SRS rates; Registrar General of India, 1991: 11-14). Thus, a high proportion of infants die before reaching their first birthday. Infant health is very important because the first year of life is crucial in laying the foundation of good health; in a normal child the highest growth (physical) occurs during the first year of life; the causes of infant deaths are largely distinct from those that operate at other ages. Infant mortality remained intractable in India in 1970's and started declining in 1980's. It is generally agreed that it is a sensitive index of health conditions of a country. If better infant health is provided, child welfare programmes will succeed. Before the infants die, they live on in malnutrition and it slowly kills the infant. Among the total infant deaths in the world, India's share of infant deaths is 27.6 per cent followed by China (9.3%) and Bangladesh (5.0%). It is only 3.0 per cent for the More Developed Countries in 1975-80 (U.N. 1984: 106).

Infant mortality rate for the world as a whole is estimated to be 70 per 1,000 live births (1985-90). The average infant mortality rate for the less developed regions is estimated to be 79 per 1,000 live births in 1985-90, about five and half times higher than for the more developed region (14 per 1,000 live births). The countries with the lowest rates are mostly in Northern and Western Europe (9 per 1,000 each), while those in Eastern and Southern Europe are with 17 per 1,000 and 15 per 1,000 respectively. Latin America has an estimated infant mortality rate of 56 per 1,000. East Asia region has a rate of 30 per 1,000 live births. But infant mortality is highest in Africa and South Asia, where rates are estimated to still exceed 100 (U.N., 1988: 36-40).

But in India, infant mortality rate is as high as 91 (1989). Moreover the rates differ widely among the various states from around 21 in Kerala to 121 in Orissa (1989). There seems to be a high infant mortality in the central belt comprising contiguous states of Gujarat (86), Rajasthan (96), Madhya Pradesh (117), U.P. (118), Orissa (121), and Bihar (91). The low infant mortality is observed in Kerala (21), Maharastra (59), and Punjab (64). Andhra Pradesh is at the intermediate stage (81). The range of infant mortality rate in rural India (1989) is around 23 in Kerala to 126 in U.P. (Registrar General of India, 1991: 23).

In India, 33 per cent of children below 5 years of age are in the category of malnourished and 5 per cent are severely malnourished. The range of malnourished and severely malnourished children in developing countries is 10-65 per cent and 1-21 per cent respectively. The corresponding figures in Bangladesh are 63 per cent and 21 per cent (1980-84) (UNICEF, 1987: 92-93).

The causes of poor health of infants are related to health and nutritional status of expectant and nursing mother, poor pre-natal and post-natal care, unsatisfactory delivery services, poverty and ignorance combined with poor mother craft, malnutrition and infestation, low maternal education, low coverage of immunisation and other health service factors, etc.

In India highest per cent of infant deaths occur within one month of birth (neo-natal mortality). Neo-natal mortality in rural area is nearly double that of urban areas (R.G. of India, 1988: 9). Pregnancies less than two years apart are a high risk for mothers and children. Having births too close together do not allow the woman's body to recover from the strain of pregnancy, child birth and breastfeeding. Furthermore, a short interval between births means that the women will have to care for several young children at the same time. Children too will suffer when they are born close together in time, when the number of children is too large, and when the mothers are too young or too old. Lack of knowledge about family planning is responsible for 'too close, too many, too young children'. Hence, children are likely to suffer from poor health, leading to impaired growth and development and are likely to die during the first year of life.

Malnutrition among expectant women is widespread in India as in other developing countries. About 30 per cent of the women in the last stages of their pregnancy have been found suffering from anaemia. Such malnutrition during pregnancy has been shown to be responsible for low birth weight and poor nutritional status of the infants and is a major factor for high infant mortality (Datta and Sarma, 1980: 217-222). In rural area of Bangladesh and Pakistan, 86 per cent and 29 per cent respectively were under absolute poverty level during 1977-84. For the same period 25 per cent and 34 per cent were under absolute poverty level in Egypt and Thailand respectively. In rural India, 51 per cent of population were under absolute poverty line (UNICEF 1987: 100-101). If this is the case, how much nutritious food they can have during pregnancy and lactation, and how much they can provide to infants? Even among the rich people, due to ignorance of the importance of nutritious foods and selection of nutritious foods, infants are suffering from poor nutrition. Some rich people feel it below their dignity to have cheap and nutritious food (eg., ragi and some green leafy vegetables), because of status symbol attached to foods. And also there is a false belief that as long as mother's milk is available, infant need not be given any additional foods. Much of the malnutrition among infants is due to this delayed starting of supplementary foods (Ramadasmurthy and Moharan, 1984: 109-110).

Due to poor health services and prevalence of poverty, pregnant women do not have sufficient ante-natal and post-natal care. In urban areas for the new born and for the infants immunisation coverage is comparatively better and satisfactory.

But in rural areas, due to low availability of health services immunisation is very less. Proper immunisation will help in reducing the incidence of infant illness and malnutrition.

Why This Study?

The Infant Mortality Rate (IMR) in India has declined considerably, especially after independence from more than 200 in 1901 to 91 in 1989. But still the rate is alarmingly high compared to even some of the developing countries, not to speak of developed countries. And moreover, as mentioned earlier there are wide regional variations in India. A number of studies have been conducted in the area of infant health and infant mortality. Anthropologists and Nutritionists mostly concentrated on anthropomological measurements and malnutrition, etc., and not focussed with many socio-economic and demographic variables. Many studies focus their attention on some aspects only, like height/weight, breast feeding, malnutrition, etc. From this, we do not get an over all picture of the determinants of poor health of infants. It needs a study from various angles like, nutrition, role of socio-economic factors, demogrpahic factors, health education, illness episode, utilisation of health services, etc., to know the causes of poor health of infants and high infant mortality and to adopt suitable socio-demographic and medical measures to reduce infant mortality rate. There is a particular necessity in a backward region like the present study area. Hence, an attempt is made in this direction in the present study. The age group 0-14 constitute child population. But in the present study among children, only infant children (0-1 age group) are examined.

Objectives of the Study

The main objectives of the study are:

1. to find out the socio-economic and cultural environment of an infant and it's mother;
2. to know the extent of knowledge that mothers have with regard to nutrition, breastfeeding, health services, etc.;
3. to assess the level of infant health through nutritional status of an infant, and the morbidity and mortality of an infant;

4. to find out determinants and differentials of an infant health;
5. to assess the mother's health and it's influence on infant health.

Hypotheses

The hypotheses to be tested in this study are:

1. Better health of the infant depends upon better economic and social conditions of parents;
2. Proper nutrition at pregnancy provides better physical development of an infant;
3. Proper nutrition for the mother at lactation period provides better physical development of an infant;
4. Health of an infant depends on breastfeeding pattern and supplementary foods;
5. Health awareness among mothers is very essential to bring forth a healthy infant;
6. The uncontrolled fertility of the mother may be responsible for the increased hazards of infection and malnutrition of the mother and child;
7. Poor obstetric care leads to poor health of the infant;
8. Health of male infant is better than that of female infant;
9. Infant health is associated with the previous history of infant mortality experienced by the mother.

Methodology

A brief description of methodology adopted for the study is given below:

1. Data Source: The data required for the study are collected by the researcher with the help of lady investigators by interviewing with a schedule, the currently married women who have at least one infant.

2. Study Area and Sampling Procedure: The study is conducted in Chittoor district of Andhra Pradesh. The Kuppam taluq of Chittoor district is chosen for actual sample survey. This taluq is chosen because it is the most backward area of

Location Map of the Study Area

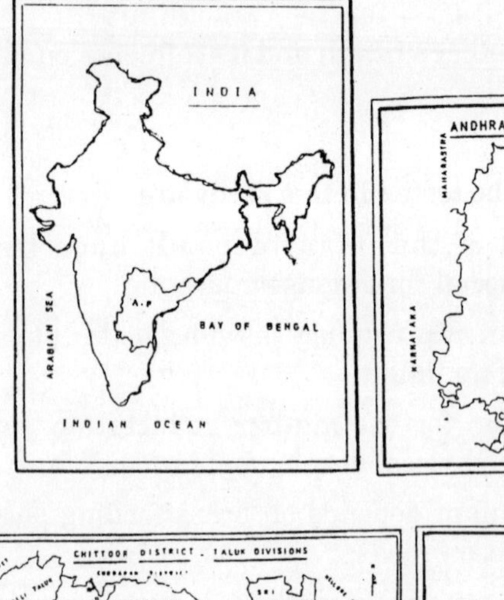

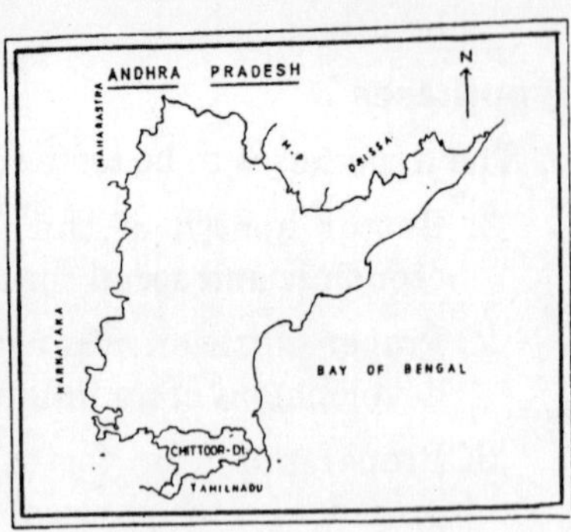

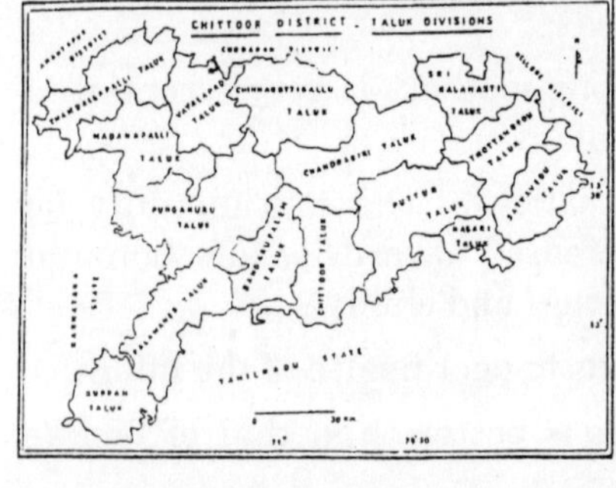

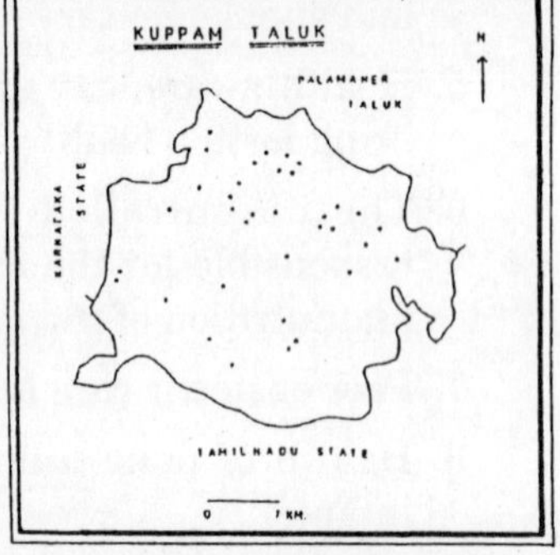

Chittoor district (Government of Andhra Pradesh, 1980: 264). Since, in a backward area like this, health status of children is very poor. There is a necessity of studying the situation of health in such an area to throw light on this problem. In the present study, only rural area is selected since the problem is more severe there. In this study, the sampling unit is a currently married woman with an infant. For selecting the sampling units, the sampling procedure adopted is as follows: At first stage, Kuppam taluq is selected purposively considering economic backwardness. The total population of Kuppam taluq is 1,36,607 according to 1981 census (Director of Census Operations, A.P. 1986: 48). We do not get figures according to 1991 census. In this, rural population constitute 1,22,958 and the remaining is urban. Kuppam town is the only urban area in this taluq. This taluq consists of 195 census villages and from these census villages, 35 census villages are selected (shown in the map) at random with the help of Table of Random Numbers. In the selected villages all currently married women with an infant are selected. If there is more than one woman with an infant in a household all such women are selected. Thus, in this study a cluster random sampling technique is used. The total sample size of 505 currently married women with an infant child are covered.

3. Schedule: The schedule is developed and utilised for the data collection. The schedule contains the following different sections:

(*a*) General particulars of the household and it's composition;

(*b*) Pregnancy history of the respondent;

(*c*) Nutrition of the mother during pregnancy and lactation;

(*d*) Health awareness of the respondent;

(*e*) Nutrition of the infant;

(*f*) Health care practices;

(*g*) Morbidity and mortality of the infant.

The conceptual model (*Figure 1.1*) that is considered in this study broadly cosists of demographic variables, socio-economic variables, nutrition and health variables and family planning variables. The conceptual model proposed here for the study of infant health is to clarify our understanding of many factors involved in determination of infant health.

1. Demographic Variables: Age at marriage of the mother, age at first conception, number of live births, still births and abortions, living children, age and sex of infants, birth order of the infant, number of infant deaths experienced by the mother, age at introduction of supplementary foods, etc.

2. Socio-economic Variables: Religion and caste, economic activity of the respondent, type of house, income, education, family size, type of family, occupation of husband and wife, bathing per week, child rearing practices, food habits, etc.

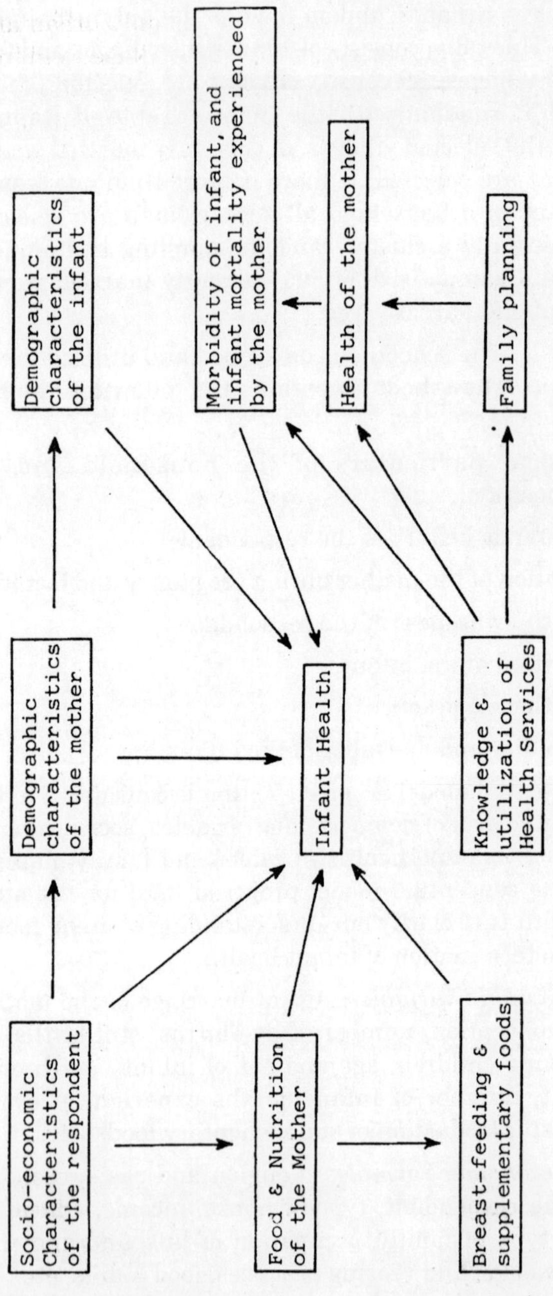

Fig. 1.1. A Conceptual Model to Infant Health

3. Nutrition and Health Variables: Height and weight of infants, additional foods taken during pregnancy and lactation, foods avoided during pregnancy and lactation, adequacy of breast milk, frequency of breastfeeding, foods 'given during first three days, supplementary foods introduced, morbidity during pregnancy, complications in post-natal period, medical check-up during pregnancy, place of delivery conducted, delivery attendant, immunisation, health services, etc.

4. Family Planning Variables: Family planning practice, reasons for practising and not practising family planning.

5. Morbidity and Mortality: Illness episodes, infant deaths experienced by the mother.

Based on the above variables about one hundred questions were asked. The survey was conducted during the period January 1989 to May 1989. After collection of data, editing is done carefully. Code design is prepared and all the data are coded. Based on the tabulation plan, different tables like uni-variate tables, bi-variate tables, and multivariate tables are prepared for analysis. Certain statistical tests like X^2-test (chi-square test), Z-test, zero order correlation analysis, and forward multiple regression analysis are applied in the analysis and interpretation of the data.

Measurement of Infant Health

Infant health can be measured in a community in terms of nutritional status, morbidity conditions (illness episode), infant mortality and also by studying milestones of an infant. Nutritional status can be assessed through clinical signs, biochemical tests, biophysical methods, and nutritional anthropometry.

Clinical examination is an important practical method for assessing the nutritional status of a community. This can be carried out by medical staff or by paramedical personnel who have been specially trained. Certain non-sampling errors like observer bias, procedural error are more in this method.

Biochemical tests of nutritional significance can be carried on a variety of body tissues, hair, muscle and bone but in practice these tests are confined to blood and urine tests. However, in rural field conditions, this will be limited by many factors like laboratory facilities, skilled laboratory staff, collection, transport, etc. Moreover, these tests are costly and time consuming to carryout.

Biophysical methods like radiographic examination, tests of physical function are rarely possible. These are not usually practically possible in survey work.

Therefore, in this study only nutritional anthropometry is considered to assess the nutritional status of an infant with the measurement of physical dimensions like body weight-for-age and body height-for-age in months. They are classified into three groups, *viz.*, normal, poor and very poor health infants as explained in subsequent paras. These are studied in relation to demographic, socio-economic, nutrition and health variables.

The morbidity conditions studied in this study are poor appetite, diarrhoea, jaundice, convulsions, conjuctivitis, bleeding from any site, measles, chickenpox, sepsis, etc. Infant mortality experienced by the respondents is also analysed with regard to the nutritional status of the present infant, and also with the other socio-economic and demographic variables. The socio-economic conditions will continue to exist even at the time of the present infant.

Standards of Reference

The anthropometric measurements obtained on infants and children are usually compared with that of a reference population. Standards for a reference population are usually obtained by measuring statistically adequate sample of a healthy, well-fed segment of the population by cross sectional method or by more time consuming longitudinal methods and measurements should be carefully made and recorded by observers. However, there are no standard anthropometric values with certainty for any community. In India, local standards of large scale studies on well-fed children are few. The data collected under the auspices of Indian Council of Medical Research (ICMR, 1972: 58-59) in different parts of the country provide valuable information for infants and children regarding community averages for weights and heights. However, they cannot be used as a reference population because these are not given for each month of infants. Therefore, it is often necessary, because of absence of local standards to use a possibly genetically less appropriate but widely available general and more often international standards. The observation that well nourished children in developing countries grow in much the same way as their counterparts in the developed world has lent support of the use of a single international standard for all (Graitcher et al. 1981: 297-299; Habitch et al. 1974: 611-615) have suggested that whatever differences there may be in the final structure, there is no evidence for ethnic difference, in growth potential during early years of life.

There are several standards available *viz.,* the measurements of Dutch children represented by Van Weiringer (1972), those of American children reported by NCHS standards, Hamill (1977), and those of British children reported by Tanner et al. (1965: 454-613), and Hardward Longitudinal Studies (Stauart and Stevenson, 1959 12-61). Among these, NCHS has provided the weights for infants, in an interval of three months. Hardward standards have given the reference weights for infants in months for both sexes combined. Reference values calculated by W.H.O. from the median reference values recommended is taken as standard of reference for the present study as they give separately for each sex and by month. (Margaret Cameron and Yougue Haffevander, 1983: 175).

Among anthropometric measurements, weight and height are excellent measures of growth in children. The other measurements—arm circumference, head and chest circumference, and skinfold thickness must be measured by personnel trained in anthropometric techniques. Among infants the measurement of weight is the method of choice for the assessment of child's state of nutrition (or health) and it has long been recognised as the most sensitive indicator of nutritional status of an infant. It is the simplest to measure accurately and the results are readily reproducible.

For measuring the weight, beam or luner scales are preferable as they are more accurate. Spring balances are not used because they easily become stretched and inaccurate from frequent use. Salter dial type spring balances have also been found to be reliable and are currently in use in ICDS areas. The same is used in the present study.

Height: In nutritional anthropometry usually only the total height is measured. While in the older children and adults, height is measured with a vertical measuring rod, in the infants and pre-school children, *i.e.,* those below the age of two years, recumbent length (crown heal length) should be measured since standing height is impossible. In the present study, total height of the infant is measured.

Classification

It is now widely agreed that the monitoring of growth and development may be the most feasible way of detecting the early stages of calamity of health in infant children. The classification of nutritional status is done differently by different researchers. Some have attached special significance to one or the other of the clinical features. Trowell (1941, 389-404) puts stress on dermatosis, Waterlow (1948) on hepatomagaly and fatty liver, Broack and Autret (1952) on red hair. Garrow, (1966, 146-154) analysed a series of cases of severe malnutrition in Jamaica taking into consideration of weight for age, odema present plus either hepatomegaly or dermatosis; Mclaren and co-workers (1967, 533-535) proposed a scoring system. Welcome classification given in Shakir paper (1972) is based on the Harvard fiftieth percentile. Another commonly used classification is Gomez (1956: 77) based on weight-for-age, and in this classification malnutrition is devided into three degrees based on Harward fiftieth standard. Jelliffe (1966) proposed a similar classification with different intervals. Bengoa (1970: 522-561) in his analysis of survey data from many countries used Gomez classification, but included in third degree malnutrition all cases with oedama regardless of body weight. Graham (1968: 107) used a method relating developmental age and chronological age.

In the present study, a child with a weight equal to or above 80 per cent of the reference weight-for-age is categorised as normals, and a weight between 79 to 60 per cent of the reference weight-for-age is categorised as poor health, and a child with a weight below 60 per cent of weight-for-age is categorised as very poor health. The details are discussed in Chapter III.

Generally, incidence of morbidity may be considered as the indicator of level of health. Since weight is the cumulative effect of exposure to morbidity (level and duration), it (weight) is considered in the present study as the index of health, and the infants are classified accordingly as mentioned above.

Plan of Report

The plan of report of the present study is as follows. This dissertation work is divided into six chapters:

Chapter I deals with introduction of the topic, objectives, hypotheses, methodology and review of literature;

In Chapter II socio-economic and demographic background of the respondents is discussed;

Chapter III is devoted to examine the interrelationship of infant health particularly with socio-economic background of the mother, demographic characteristics of the mother, demographic characteristics of the infant, food and nutrition of the mother and child, health of the mother, health services and family planning;

Chapter IV deals with morbidity and mortality of infants. It is also discussed in relation to other socio-economic and demographic factors;

In *Chapter V,* prediction of infant health is analysed with the technique of Forward Regression Analysis;

Chapter VI gives an overview of the study. In this chapter, summary of findings is presented and the remedial measures are recommended.

REVIEW OF LITERATURE

As a preliminary step, a review of literature was undertaken to determine to what extent the research questions had already been answered by others; to find research gaps and generate research hypothesis for the study; to improve research design on the basis of the experience of other investigators; to facilitate the interpretation of the results of the present study and their comparison with those of previous ones; and to systematise and facilitate access to the growing and diversified body of literature touching on the subject 'Infant Health'. Research on Infant health in India has made important and rapid strides forward in the past decade.

There are a number of studies that are related to infant health. The important variables considered by them are reviewed in the present section, such as education, income, age at marriage and age at first conception, food habits and food taboos, infant's physical growth, malnutrition of the child, pre-lacteal meal, breast-feeding, weaning, birth order, birth spacing, health services, family planning, health education, illness episode and infant mortality, etc.

Education

Education of father and mother has positive association on infant health and the importance of education particularly of the mother has been well established and widely accepted. Better education for women is now a familiar health slogan. Caldwell's analysis of survey data from Ibadan, Nigeria demonstrated that mother's education was a more decisive determinant of child survival than other family characteristics such as husband's occupation and education (Caldwell, 1979). The association between mother's education and infant survival is confirmed by a study conducted in India also, (Srinivasan, *et al.,* 1985).

The level of female education shows a strong negative influence on infant mortality. A study conducted in India showed that the infant mortality among mothers with no education was estimated to be 145 deaths per 1000 births. It decreased to 101 among mothers with some education and to 71 among mothers with atleast primary education. These results imply a 50 per cent reduction in infant mortality with at least primary school education. (Anrudh, 1988; 142).

National study for India in 1979 (Ministry of Home Affairs, 1983) and China in 1982 (Yang and Davidlf, 1985) confirmed the negative association between mother's education and risk of death in infancy.

Cochrane, 0 'Hara and Leslie assembled data from 33 countries, including ten from the World Fertility Survey (WFS)

(Cochrane, *et al.*, 1980). The United Nations conducted an analysis of survey data from 15 countries of which seven were WFS surveys. (U.N. 1985). Both the above revealed a linear relationship between maternal education and childhood mortality with an average 7 to 9 per cent decline in mortality ratios with each one year increment in mother's education.

Mother's education helps to improve infant health because educated mothers are likely to be better nourished, more willing to ignore harmful food taboos during pregnancy, and less subject to heavy manual work during pregnancy than their less educated counterparts (John and Jerome, 1989).

Income

Poverty affects all aspects of life including health, illness and related behaviour. Poverty among villages in India never allows the female members in the household to take any special food or supplementary food during pregnancy or in the period when she breast-feeds her child, and this will affect the infant health (Khan, 1986: 8). A study conducted in New Delhi showed that the infants with poor nutrition belonging to lower socio-economic classes were shorter and higher than their counterparts from the higher socio-economic classes (Datta Bonik, 1977: 147). And also in an Indian study it is found that malnourished and severely malnourished infants are more in lower socio-economic classes (Sengupta, 1971: 46). A study conducted in urban slum of Hyderabad revealed that the growth of infant born to mother of low socio-economic status was slightly lesser than standard in the first three months of life and with increasing age of the infant the growth faltering increase (Madhunath and Geervani, 1979: 422-428).

A number of studies showed that 40-50 per cent of the population in rural U.P. live below the poverty line and do not get the minimum required calorie intake and this will have an adverse effect on health of infants. (Khan, 1988: 238).

Age at Marriage and Age at Motherhood

Age at marriage has an impact on the health of the women through age at birth of first child and in turn has an impact on the health of an infant. Parents (mostly in rural areas) perform the marriage of their children, particularly daughters soon after their puberty or even earlier due to various reasons such as social custom, to satisfy the grand parents, dowry problem, availability of suitable match and to dispose of the responsibility. But this may effect the health of the woman since physically and mentally she may not be matured, and may also result in early pregnancy, abortions, premature births, still births and live births and reflect on the health of the women.

Throughout the world, women who marry late in their mid or upper twenties tend to have fewer children than women who marry early. Fewer children ensure better health of children (Population Reports, Series M, 1979).

If women postpone marriage and motherhood from age 16 to age 19, motherhood from 18 to 21, then they can enter marriage and motherhood with greater emotional and physical maturity to meet the challenges of family life. One of the challenges of life is bringing up healthy children. In this review, the limitation is that there are no studies available which interrelate age at marriage and infant health.

Food Habits

Pregnant and lactating women require more calories, proteins and other nutrients than other women. Nutritional requirements are greater for lactating women than pregnant women.

As recommended by the National Institute of Nutrition, additional daily allowance of a pregnant woman is 200 calories and 20 gms protein, and that of a lactating woman is 1000 calories and 40 gms protein (Protein Foods and Nutrition Development Association of India, 1973: 59).

A proper diet intake of a pregnant and lactating mother is very important for a healthy infant. The more poorly nourished the women the longer should be inter-pregnancy interval. If another pregnancy follows too rapidly, her nutritional level will be deficient, resulting in low weight gain during pregnancy, severe anaemia, high rates of both maternal and peri-natal mortality and low weight of offspring (Population Reports, 1975). In developing countries the main problem during pregnancy and lactation is malnutrition.

The information about food intake of pregnant and lactating women is scanty. The main diet of pregnant and lactating woman in Andhra Pradesh is cereals (rice) and pulses. Cereals are consumed more than pulses. Most of the woman take two meals daily in a rural area and three meals daily in an urban area. Milk is rarely used in rural area and is only used in tea or coffee in urban area. Eggs and fruits are often used only as festival foods. Both in nature and amount the food eaten by pregnant and lactating mother does not differ appreciably.

In India, observations on food intake reveal that a woman takes her food only after she has served all the family members. Usually what remains are the left overs which many a times are inadequate to provide the minimum calorie intake. In Uttar Pradesh, most of the times the food in the family consists of chapathis and one vegetable. Occassionally, they do have pulses but milk is hardly consumed. However, a small amount of milk is taken if the family owns cattle and if it milchs. Milk is rarely purchased for anybody and the question does not arise about the women drinking it even if she is pregnant or lactating (Khan, *et. al.,* 1986: 7-9).

A study conducted in Varanasi, U.P. in India, among 184 pregnant, 95 lactating and 20 non-pregnant women, it was revealed that the dietary intake is below the recommendation of the Indian Council of Medical Research (ICMR, 1977). The intake of rural pregnant women was lower than those of urban pregnant women. The rural lactating women lost body weight about 1.2 kg during lactation, probably owing to their heavy daily work. (Bhatia, *et. al.,* 1981). It could also be due to poor nutritional level of mothers.

Anaemia is one of the most frequently observed disease in the world today (anaemia is a health problem, but is classified as a disease according to W.H.O Inter-national Classification of Diseases). It is specially prevalent among young children, pregnant and lactating women. Low birth weight babies or even infant mortality is the consequence of malnutrition among pregnant women (U.N. 1981: 1). Malnutrition among poor pregnant women in India is also widespread. Over 30 per cent of these women in the last 4 stage of their pregnancy have been found suffering from severe anaemia (Gopalan, 1974). In South India, it was found that 43 per cent pregnant women were suffering from malnutrition (Gopalan and Vijaya Raghavan, 1971: 2). A study conducted in the field practice villages of the department of Preventive and Social Medicine, Banaras Hindu University in Uttar Pradesh, among 232 pregnant women 174 (75.0%) had anaemia (Luwang and Gupta, 1980: 414). In a study of 113 families in Phillippine pregnant and lactating women generally followed the family meal pattern and only 21 took vitamin or mineral supplements. They did not add special foods to their usual diet though 15 reported craving for particular foods (Opena, *et al.,* 1977: 114-119).In Bolivia, women do not consume extra foods during lactation (International Communication Service, 1983). In Eucador, about 40 per cent of pregnant and lactating women have some degree of malnutrition. Staple food in the country includes bananas, yucca, wheat, tubers, corn and potatoes. Few women report dietary changes during pregnancy (International Communication Service, 1982). In 1977, a prospective study in Kenya indicate that Kansa women generally take tea with milk and sugar at breakfast with full meals around midday and late in the evening. No change in meal pattern or type of dishes was observed during pregnancy and lactation. The most regularly eaten foods were maize, legumes, milk, fat and sugar. The energy and nutrient intake of pregnant woman was considerably lower than that of lactating woman (Kusian, *et al.,* 1984). The dietary pattern of the mothers is reviewed, but studies are not available establishing the relationship between mother's nutrition and infant health. In my study an attempt is made in this direction.

Food Taboos

Food taboos have their influence on nutritional status. There are religious and cultural taboos also. Muslims avoid pork. Similar taboos against mutton, snails, goats, and beef exist in other religious groups.

A study was conducted in the urban ICDS block, Tirupati, Chittoor district and in the rural ICDS block, Kambam, Anantapur district in Andhra Pradesh. About 76 per cent rural mothers and 20 per cent urban mothers were afraid of eating many food items like jaggery, lemon, mango, onion, cucumber, fish, ghee, curd, coconut, brinjal, etc. During lactation as they felt it would lead to a gastric problem among babies or would harm them (Indira Bai, *et. al.,* 1981: 277-280). This superstition is also present in other parts of the country.

About 76 per cent in the rural area of Rewa, Madhya Pradesh, had this idea in contrast to 20 per cent in the urban area. One or many of the following items were taboo: brinjal, coconut, chillies, cold water, curd, cucumber, dhal, drumstick, drinking water, fish, ghee, ice cream or ice water, jaggery, lemon, mango, onion, oil foods, pumpkin, potato, sugar and tomato (Gurudev, *et al.,* 1982).

In Berhampur (Orissa) during confinement and 4-6 months after, the mother had to avoid certain foods such as sea fish, dried fish, meat, red gram, potato, red pumpkin, colocosia, fermented rice and sour dishes. (Alabi, 1984).

After delivery, many prefer to take foods of animal origin like meat, fish, eggs, milk and milk products as they are considered to be good for health. Some foods are avoided during the post-natal period in different regions in India: Hyderabad region, bringal, cluster beans, potato, gourds; New Delhi region some foods like tamarind, lemon and pickles, lussy and curds, fried and spicy foods, rice, black gram, bengal gram, etc; and in West Bengal region fish, meat, egg, onions, mustard oil, pumpkin; and in Coimbatore region cholam or ragi, jack fruit, egg, mango, drumsticks, etc. This preferencial food consumption practices could be traced to certain culturally determined beliefs, systems associated with community concept of hot and cold foods. Some of the foods are avoided thinking that they are producing cold and lead to stiff joints and paralysis of limbs. Some foods are believed to be hard to digest and therefore cause gastro-intestinal disturbances not only in mothers but also in their breast-fed infants (ICMR, 1984: 5-10).

Food taboos are observed in some other countries also. From a study conducted at the Ibe-Ife University teaching hospital in Nigeria between December, 1978 and May, 1979, it was observed that 83.5 per cent of mothers believed that meat and fish would cause intestinal worm and stomach pain. Interestingly 69.6 per cent believed that eating eggs would make a child steal (Jinadu, *et al.,* 1986). There are harmful food habits due to certain cultural customs and it has a deliterious effect on health. Such habits are the failure to give young children fish (Malaya), the use of pepper water enemas (West Africa), forced hand feeding (Nigeria), opium sedation of infants (India), extreme dietary restrictions in pregnancy (Burma) (Williams, and Jelliffe, 1976: 26). Irrational behaviour and harmful practices are found in all cultures, and these will effect the health of the infant, but there are no studies that interrelate food taboos and infant health.

Physical Growth of Infants

Nutritional health in early childhood needs monitoring by measurements of at least weight, height, head circumference, chest circumference, arm circumference and triceps skinfold.

Essentially, all children in India are breast-fed and do well for about 4 months, after which two types of findings appear; average growth increments drop significantly below Harvard standards and a high rate of morbidity is evident at fourth month of age (Desweemer, *et al.,* 1983: 126-156).

Data on nutrtional anthropometry of hundred breast-fed Indian infants in rural area near Hyderabad city were compared with those of Harvard infants. Growth of exclusively breast-fed infants was about same as that of Harvard infants upto about 6 months old, but was impaired later with increased incidence of mild and moderate forms of growth retardation (Rao and Ram, 1982: 307-317). Another study conducted in a slum area of Hyderabad revealed that mean weights of infants showed a progressive increase from birth to five months. Beyond five months, there was a faltering in the weight curve. While the infants doubled their birth weight at fourth month, they did not show a tripling even at the age of one year (Leela Raman, *et al.,* 1989: 195-205).

A study conducted in Tamilnadu revealed that the mean weight for both boys and girls every month recorded a consistant increase during twelve months, except between 9th and 10th month. The birth weight (2.82 kgs) doubled at

4 months (5.64 kgs) and tripled by one and half years (Rajammal, *et al.,* 1977: 361). In Delhi area Shantighosh, *et al.,* observed that male infants are heavier than female infants.

In Haryana, sixtytwo infants with birth weight more than 2.5 kg following normal delivery were followed up for physical growth in weight until 6 months of age with exclusive breastfeeding. Mean weight increased from 2.94 kg at birth to 7.70 kg at 6th month. Males were heavier throughout than female infants. Maternal parity and education had no influence on growth (Kumari *et al.,* 1982: 963-968). In a cohort study of 200 infants over a period of one year in Uttar Pradesh revealed that the nutritional status of infants upto 6 months of age was significantly better than of infants more than 6 months of age (Hasan, *et al.,* 1991: 84-86).

The weight and height of well-to-do Indian children were found to be essentially similar to those of American children upto 14 years of age, (Vijaya Raghavan, 1971: 648). These data suggest that the genetic potential for growth of Indian children is similar to that of children from Western countries. The growth failure observed among many children in our rural communities will therefore appear to be due to environmental and nutritional factors. Other studies have also shown that the pattern of growth and development of well-to-do Indian infants was similar to those of Harvard (Datta Banik, *et al.,* 1970: 135-142). Weights were measured for 2026 healthy Thai children of good socio-economic status from birth to six years old. During the first six months of life measurements were comparable with those of North American infants, but after six months, growth curves for Thai children fell below those of North Americans (Khanjanasthaiti, P., *et al.,* 1973: 88-100).

In an ideal situation where both mother and infant are well nourished and healthy, breast milk alone will usually enable growth parallel to all established references upto 3 months. But between 3 to 6 months the growth will have small deviation from some established references (Sewaed and Serdula, 1984: 759).

The faltering of growth which frequently occurs in infants at about three months old in developing countries is some times attributed to insufficient food or to increased exposure to infection.

Malnutrition

Malnutrition is one of the world's most common health problem and it is widespread in developing countries, especially among young children. Malnutrition causes death directly. More often it reduces resistence to infectious diseases and so, while the impact is hard to measure, it contributes mortality right from first year of life. In addition infant malnutrition inhibits later growth and development (Wincoff, *et al.,* 1980: 171-176).

Earlier studies revealed that in rural India mal-nurishment among infants is prevalent to an extent varying from 20 to 40 per cent (weight less than 80 per cent of 50th per centile of Harvard standard level indicates malnutrition) (Urmila Sharma, 1987: 111-118).

In a survey conducted in Trivandrum, it is found that among infants (Weight-for-age) 25.0 per cent of them are normal, 49.6 per cent mild, 19.5 per cent moderate and the remaining 5.9 per cent severely malnourished (Ragimol Cherian, *et al.,* 1988: 84). And also in a study conducted in Uttar Pradesh revealed that about 65.5 per cent below six months of age had normal nutrition compare to 32.4 per cent of infants above six months of age. At the end of one year, only 15 per cent infants had normal nutritional status, 36.5 per cent infants had grade-I malnutrition, 36.0 per cent infants grade-II malnutrition. Further, 5.0 per cent had grade-III and 1.5 per cent had grade-IV malnutrition (Hasan, and Khan, 1991: 84-86).

In India, nutritional status of children studied are mostly for '0-6' age group (pre-school children) and not seperately for infants. In Andhra Pradesh, as high as 90 per cent of pre-school children are deficient in calories, either with or without protein adequacy (Vijayaraghavan and Rao, 1973: 31). A study conducted in West Bengal revealed that out of 632 children (0-6 age) 76 per cent were found to be suffering from different degrees of malnutrition (Ghosh, 1986: 1).

Another study was conducted in 10 randomly selected anganwadi of the Tribal ICDS block Garhi, Rajasthan. The 50th per cent of the Harvard standard was used to assess the nutritional status of children (0-6 age). The proportion of normal children is found to be 36.9 per cent. The proportion of Grade I, Grade II, Grade III, Grade IV malnourished children are 23.8 per cent, 25.3 per cent, 10.9 per cent and 2.9 per cent respectively. (Bhandari, *et al.,* 1981: 187-188).

Another study was conducted in the rural ICDS block Kathma, Haryana. The nutritional status of children (0-6) is found to be about 34.0 per cent normal. The proportion of Grade I, II, III and IV malnourished children are 24.0 per cent, 23.7 per cent, 12.0 per cent and 6.1 per cent respectively (Sundar Lal., 1980: 293-296).

The base line survey was conducted in 1981 in the urban ICDS block, Pune, Maharastra. The proportion of normal children is found to be 32.3 per cent. Grade I and Grade II malnourished children are 33.7 per cent and 26.2 per cent respectively. Grade III and Grade IV malnourished children combined together is 7.8 per cent (Mahendar., *et al.,* 1985: 1-7).

A study was conducted in the rural ICDS block, Kathma, Haryana, The proportion of normal children (0-6 age) is 51.6 per cent, 30.7 per cent in Grade I, 14.6 per cent in Grade II, 1.7 per cent and 0.4 per cent in Grade III and Grade IV respectively (Sunder Lal., 1985: 23-28).

Studies in 25 developing countries have found that malnutrition is most common after six months of life (Keller, *et al.,* 1983: 129-168). A study conducted in Turkey jointly by Ministry of Health, Turkey and UNFPA showed that the number of undernourished infants is much higher after 6 months of age where the infants do not get enough food (Muftu, 1981: 41-45).

A nutritional survey of infants was conducted in four villages of the North-East Brazilian state of Pernambuco in 1983. In terms of Gomez weight for-age classification, 50.3 per cent of the infants over 3 months old were found to be malnourished with 17.9 per cent exhibiting Grade II or Grade III malnutrition (Lucia de Freitas, *et al.,* 1986: 138-146). From various studies in India, it is observed that the prominent causes of malnutrition are attributed to factors like socio-economic conditions, feeding babies with diluted milk, ignorance of special needs of infants, inappropriate cultural beleifs and practices, etc.

Prelacteal Meal

In majority of cases, women delay the initiation of breast-feeding by as much as two or three days because they believe that the initial milk is not good for the new-borns. Valuable colostrum is discarded.

There are also widespread practices of introducing prelacteal feeds. Both these practices increase the risk of infection. Although there is no empirical information about the effect of these practices on infant mortality, changes in these practices are most likely to increase the chances of child survival. The prelacteal feeds consists of some herbal cancoctions called Gutti in several parts of India often mixed with ghee or honey or even castor oil. This feed is believed to cleanse the infant's system. Plain water with honey, sugar or joggery, and in urban areas with glucose is a normal prelacteal feed (Leela Visaria, 1988: 87).

A study conducted in Uttar Pradesh revealed that Gutti was given as the first feed by 94 per cent of mothers and honey by 3 per cent of mothers. Almost all mothers felt that Gutti is essential to clean the intestines of the baby and that colostrum is dirty and harmful and should therefore be discarded (Hansan, *et al.*, 1991: 84-86).

Infant feeding in Simla-Hills (India) have been studied in 600 families. Prelacteal feeds given to babies included honey (43.6%), Ghutti (11.5%) glucose water (9.6%), water and milk (8.3%), and no feed (25.5%). On the second day 83 per cent of the mothers began breastfeeding(Bansal, 1973: 1869-1875).

Mothers of 800 randomly selected infants belonging to Berhampur, South of Orissa, India were studied by Simpson (1984). In 73 per cent of cases prelacteal feeding was initiated due to over anxiety for feeding the baby immediately after birth. This included very diluted cow's milk, sugar candy water, and diluted mixture of honey and water. Sometimes prelacteal feeding was given with a piece of cotton plug and torn old cloth soaked with the feeding formula and squeezed into the baby's mouth (Simpson, 1984: 1024-1029).

Prelacteal feeds fill a baby's stomach, reduced his/her appetite, and make the baby less willing to suck at the breast. This deals the onset of lactation and increases the dangers of engorgement. If a baby is given his/her prelacteal feeds (or later feeds) from a bottle with a rubber teat, he/she is likely to develop 'nipplex confusion' and fail to suck effectively from his/her mouth (Kings, 1984). Therefore, the infant should be put to the breast preferably in the labour room but definetely within 4 hours after delivery. Normal newborns do not require any type of prelacteal feed with glucose or artificial milk as colostrum is enough to meet the limited needs of the newborn baby in the first few days of life (Indian Academy of Paediatrics, 1984).

Breast-feeding

The importance of proper breast-feeding for healthy infant has been well recognised. There are many benefits of breast-feeding, and they are: breast milk provides some immunological protection for the infant, infant nutritional needs are best satisfied, breast-feeding costs nothing as against feeding with substitutes, breast-feeding is an important means of birth spacing, provides a close relationship between mother and child, avoides dental carries caused by children sleeping with bottles in their mouths, promotes greater intellectual ability (Population Reports, 1981). An appropriate breast-feeding practice is the single most important factor for an infant's growth and survival. It is the best and physiologically feasible for the great majority of women. For mothers breast-feeding helps both to stop uterine bleeding and promote a better flow of milk.

A longitudinal study 25 years ago demonstrated that exclusively breast-fed infants had satisfactory growth through four months but thereafter many mothers were unable to produce the 950 ml of milk required to sustain a healthy infant weighing 6 kg, the average for a four month old (Vega Franco, *et al.*, 1984).

Studies in breast-feeding indicate that the incidence of infection related mortality is significantly lower among breast-fed children than formula fed. This is perhaps, because of the immunological protection provided by breast-feeding. (Khan, 1991: 39-50; Kasasree, *et al.*, 1982: 281-284; Devdas, *et al.*, 1977: 361-365). In Denmark, the growth of 50 infants given breast milk during the first three months was compared with 50 infants given bovine milk. All the growth pattern were significantly better in the breast-fed groups than the artificially fed. Morbidity from diarrhoea and upper respiratory infection was higher in the bovine milk group than the breast-fed. It also revealed that breast-fed infants had overall morbidity rates 4 to 16 per cent lower than infants fed exclusively artificially (Biering-Serensen, *et al.,* 1983: 36-4). A study conducted in Shanghai showed that breast-fed infants under six month old grow better than the artificially fed (Shanghai Health Care Coordinating Groupe, 1974: 604-608).

As is known in India, breast-feeding is universal and prolonged. A study conducted in Prakasam district of Andhra Pradesh revealed that considerably higher proportion of women (73.5%) breast-fed their children for more than one year. And also as can be expected this proportion is considerably higher in rural area (83.0%) than in urban area (Lakshmamma, 1991: 172-76).

A study conducted in Uttar Pradesh, showed that about 55-60 per cent of women in the study villages breast-fed 20 or more months and the child was fed on his/her demand. (Khan, 1986: 14).

A prospective fertility survey was carried out by the Gandhigram Institute of Rural Health and Family Planning. Three thousand households are selected from Atloor block. The average lactation period was 21.65 months in the area. (Krishnamurthy, 1970: 12).

Mothers of 800 randomly selected infants belonging to Berhampur, South Orissa, India, were interviewed. Among the breast-fed infants, about 97 per cent of them were breast-fed even after the age of 6 months (Simpson, 1984: 1024-1029). Similar pattern is found in other Asian countries. The percentage of children breast-fed ranges from 74 per cent in Malaysia to 98 per cent in Nepal. In developing countries as a whole the duration ranges from 18-24 months in rural areas to less than a year, and often as little as 3 months in urban areas. The duration of breast-feeding is longer in Africa and Asia than in Latin America and Carribbean. It varies according to socio-economic and demographic conditions (Ahamed, 1984: 21-31).

A survey was conducted to assess prevalence and duration of breast-feeding on Kuwait women who are willing to furnish data. The results show that 71 per cent of newborns are breast-fed at birth. The percentage of breast-fed infants declines to 58 per cent by the time they are one month old, and to 10 per cent among five month old infants. The expected duration of breast-feeding (average) is two months (Al-Bustan, 1986: 135-148).

The information on prevalance and duration of breast-feeding in South America, is available. Prevalence figures for Middle America range from 75 per cent for Costa-Rica (mean duration 20 months) to above 90 per ent of Guatemala (mean duration 18-24 months); the range in Carribbean is 80 per cent in Trinidad-Tobago (6 to 8 months mean duration), to 90 per cent in St. Kitts-Nevis (6-8 months mean duration). The highest prevalence in South America is found in Paraguay and Peru (92 per cent with 11-12 months mean duration). The 1973 epidemiological study found that 52 per cent of infants in Mexico city were still breast-fed at 6 months (Vega Franco, *et al.,* 1984: 630-635). The information on prevalence of breast-feeding in Europe is also available. The prevalence of breast-feeding in England and Wales was 62 per cent in 1983, representing 11 per cent increase since 1975. Scandinavian countries have a higher prevalence, variously estimated at 45 per cent to 83 per cent. In Western Europe breast-feeding prevalance ranges from 32 per cent in Belgium to 92 per cent in Switzerland (Gussla, *et al.,* 1984).

The prevalance in United States in 1983 is estimated at 61.4 per cent with 27.3 per cent of infants currently being breast-fed at 5-6 months. By contrast, in the United States, Sweden, and Australia breast-feeding is being more prevalent, especially among educated women, although the average length of breast-feeding remains short (Population Reports, 1981: 527-532).

Duration of (full or partial) breast-feeding is frequently and negatively associated with high socio-economic status and maternal health, urban residence, high maternal education and income, oral contraceptive use and maternal work away from home. Duration of breast-feeding is also negatively associated with increasing maternal age and parity. The regional exception to the association with maternal age appears in Africa (Forman, 1984: Ahmed, *et al.,* 1984).

In recent years many developing countries have experienced a steep decline in breast-feeding. The decline is more common in large towns and cities, but similar trends are also present in rural areas. In most developing countries, almost all women breast-fed their children initially, but there is evidence that the length of breast-feeding is declining, especially in urban areas (Population Reports, 1981: 527-532). Younger mothers stop breast-feeding sufficientely early to retain their physique and appearance (Krishnamurthy, 1970: 12).

Nortzan has evaluated trends in breast-feeding in some Asian and Latin American countries; Taiwan, Malaysia, Korea, Singapore, Thailand, Mexico, and Panama. A downward trend in breast-feeding exists in most of the seven countries. The pattern of decline varies markedly from country to country. In Taiwan and Malaysia, both the proportion of infants ever breast-fed and the duration of breast-feeding has declined markedly. In Thailand most of the decline is due to reduction in the duration of nursing with little change noted in the proportion of infants ever breast-fed. A considerable reduction in the longer duration of breast-feeding accounts for most of Korea's decline. In Panama, the decline in nursing is based on breast-feeding duration. Contradictory patterns are found in Mexico with a small decline in the proportion of infants ever breast-fed off set by inconsistent change in the proportion of infants breast-fed at different ages. The pattern of change in Singapore resembles the recent trend in breast-feeding in developing countries, *i.e.,* sharp decline in the proportion of infants ever breast-fed and in shorter nursing durations, followed by an upturn in both measures. Despite the common belief that most breast-feeding change has occured among urban populations, declines are noted in the rural areas of several countries (Nortzon, 1984: 648-666).

In most European countries, the incidence of breast-feeding declined spectacularly during the present century. Support groups have been formed in 8 countries in Northern Europe since 1968 to encourage breast-feeding. Most are lay groups consisting of women with experience in breast-feeding, who are able to give advice on the physiology and problems associated with the practice. Activities are varied, *e.g.*, classes, counselling in maternity wards, information sessions for the public and health professionals, news letters. Breast-feeding counsellors must have experienced in breast-feeding. In the Federal Republic of Germany, 350 groups act independently and training is informal, but the average duration of breast-feeding increased from 6.5 to 9.1 weeks from 1980-1984, and the number of babies breast-fed at 6 months increased from 2 per cent to 10 per cent (Brunn, 1986: 65-68).

Huffman's reasons for changes in breast-feeding behaviour are social, cultural and economic influence on parental attitudes and behaviour in relation to self-images. Health care services in most developing countries also have been associated with lower rates of initiation of breast-feeding and shorter durations (Huffman, 1984-: 170-183).

Reasons most often given for discontinuation of breast-feeding include discomfort, subsequent pregnancy, a feeling that the child is too old to be breast-fed, the mother being too busy, illness of the mother or the child, insufficient flow of breast milk, and the child's death (Ahmed, *et al.*, 1984).

Bottle feeding is treated as a symbol of sophistication having high prestige value. Breast engorgement, sore and cracked nipple are common complaints which some times come women to stop breast-feeding (Population Reports, 1981: 527-532). Women may also believe that breast-feeding will change the shape and size of the breast, although this has not been proved.

To test the attitude of mothers to breast-feeding a sample of 649 breast-feeders were interviewed 12 months after delivery in Wales. Interms of their enjoyment, 63 per cent of mothers said that breast-feeding is enjoyable and it was higher among mothers having previous experience with breast-feeding and those experiencing fewer problems *e.g.*, sore breasts, engorgement. Sore breasts and engorgement were experienced by 51 per cent. The majority of mothers (81%) said that they would breast-feed their next child; only 15 per cent said that they would not (Jones, 1986).

Weaning

Weaning period is an extremely important period of childhood from the point of infant health. Weaning is a process that begins with the first introduction of foods in addition to breast milk and continues untill breast-feeding is terminated and the child is fully integrated into the family diet. Termination of breast-feeding may be gradual or abrupt.

Supplementary foods are given to infants as early as one month to two months or as late as 18 months. It has been documented that too early introduction of supplements under conditions of poor environmental sanitation is likely to increase infective morbidity, and mortality (Wyon and Gordon, 1971; O'Malley, *et al.*, 1968). Delaying the introduction of supplements too late is likely to cause undernutrition (Waterstar, 1984; 1971; Water Loo, 1981; Wyon and Gorden, 1971). Breast milk is sufficient to support adequate growth in majority of infants upto six months (Whitehead, 1981: 168; Chandran, 1981; Ahn, 1979).

Exclusive breast-feeding may not be adequate to sustain growth beyond the first 5 to 6 months of life. Therefore, supplementary feeding with energy food mixtures containing adequate amounts of nutrients such as proteins, fats, iron and vitamins should be introduced 4 to 5 months age without stopping breast-feeding (Ghai, 1985: 3).

A majority of women from developed countries and women belonging to middle and upper income groups in developing countries start introduction of supplements from about third month (Prema Ramachandran, 1983). A study was conducted in Lalganj, Rae Bareli district, Uttar Pradesh. The average age at weaning was 15.4 months, (Gupta, *et al.*, 1984: 368). Another study conducted in Madhya Pradesh revealed that age at weaning was 13-15 months and 10-12 months for the rural and urban infants respectively (Patodi, *et al.,* 1976: 333-338).

A study conducted in urban slums of Hyderabad revealed that a poor performance of growth during the latter part of infancy is a reflection of improper weaning and inadequate consumption of supplementary foods. (Madhunath and Geervani, 1979: 422-428). A study on 250 infants was conducted in rural and urban communities near Indore, India that 18.4 per cent and 12.8 per cent of the infants showed signs of severe malnourishment after the age of six months. This is due to delayed weaning and diluted cow's or buffallows milk (Patodi *et al.,* 1976: 333-338).

In India, regarding types of weaning food given also vary widely depending on the products locally available. The most common pattern of weaning is to introduce a baby cereal, usually wheat base or rice base. This is followed by tinned, bottled, or dehydrated baby foods, rusks, biscuits, bread, etc.

A study was conducted in the urban ICDS block, Tirupati, Chittoor district and in the rural ICDS block Kambadur, Anantapur district in Andhra Pradesh. In rural and urban block the sample size was 500 each. Many infants in the rural area were fed exclusively on cereals. The other supplementary foods were pulses, egg occasionally and mutton once a month (Indira bai, 1981: 277-280). A study conducted by Lakshmamma in Prakasam district of Andhra Pradesh revealed that only about 11.4 per cent of women started giving weaning foods to their children at 6th month or less. Generaly rice is given at 6th month to the infant if she/he agrees to take rice they will give only that, otherwise they give buffallow milk, now and then rice. Other types of foods given are tinned milk, Farex, biscuits, etc., (Lakshmamma, *et al.,* 1991: 44; Indira Bai 1981: 277-280).

A study on mothers of 800 randomly selected infants belonging to Berhampur, South Orissa, India, were interviewed to know infant feeding practices at the community level. Supplementary feeding was initiated at an early age (second or third month) mainly because the mother felt that she had inadequate lactation and partly because she presumed that early supplementation would lead to better growth of her baby.

Yet, the supplementary feeding formula was very much diluted (Satpathy, *et al.*, 1984: 207-212). In a study of feeding practices in rural and urban area of Himachal Pradesh (India), it was found that almost all children were breast-fed and the supplementary foods were diluted and urban women tended to introduce supplementary milk feeds earlier than rural women (Datta, 1984.) .

Infant feeding practices were studied in 500 tribal families covering about a population of 2566 in Pooli Block, Kulu District, Himachal Pradesh. About 92 per cent of the children aged 13-24 months received semi-solids mainly as Attu and Chulilaphi (boiled) dried appricot with Attu, salt, spice and oil. Solid and dried food was introduced as early as 6 months (Bahe, 1979: 337-341).

In a nine country study by W.H.O on breast-feeding revealed that, more than half of the urban Indian women were regularly supplementing diets at the age of two to three months, compared with only two per cent of the rural women. In Ethiopia, 12 per cent of urban poor still had not begun food supplementation as late as 18 months. (W.H.O. 1983). Regarding the practice of the supplementary food to child at 6-7 months, 6 per cent of the infants in the Ethopian urban poor group, 78 per cent in Indian urban poor, and 88 per cent in the Indian rural group are receiving no substantial addition to breast milk. Other groups in which relatively high proportion of women were not regularly giving any supplementary foods were the Guatemala rural group and the Indian middle income group, (W.H.O. 1981). In Thailand, a large proportion of rural children are not weaned for atleast a year (John Knodel and Nibhan Debavlya, 1980). Breast-feeding in Bolivia usually lost over a year may extend to 3-4 years. Supplements like coffee, tea, soups, and potatoes are introduced at about six months. As a substitute for unavailable breast milk bottle feeding using oats, corn, coffee, or tea are used (International Nutrition Communication Services, 1983).

To obtain information on weaning methods in infant welfare clinics in Ilo-Ife, Nigeria a study of the 65 women was conducted,; 32.4 per cent gave their infants, sweets, biscuits and bottles each time the child asked for the breast. They adopted different methods to discourage the child from breast-feeding. Twenty nine per cent applied bitter leaf or other sour leaf on their nipples. Fifteen per cent of the women placed cotton wool on top of the nipple to frighten the children and 10.0 per cent reported the use of sedative drugs of alcohol such as phenergen at night (Elegbe, 1981: 261-265).

Infant feeding practices among 353 Bedovin families in transition from semi-nomadic to settlement conditions in the Negev area of Israel were compared with those of 302 Jewish families from the same area. Rice was the first solid food to be introduced to Bedovin infants, while fruits and vegetables were the first solids introduced to the Jewish infants. Rice was not an important constituent of the diet of Jewish infants. By age six months, 93 per cent of the Jewish infants were eating fruits and vegetables, 78 per cent meat, 49 per cent bread and 53 per cent eggs, in contrast to 20 per cent, 13 per cent, 8 per cent and 18 per cent among the Bedovins. Bedovin infants feeding practices resembled those prevalent among rural population in developing countries (Dagan, *et al.,* 1984: 1029-34).

Most mothers in India, believe that the infant should eat sweet food before they eat salty foods. Mothers believe that the 'hot' foods are bad to children. Infants are often weaned suddenly due to new pregnancy, illness of the mother, insufficient milk, or the mothers work (International Nutrition Communication Service, 1982). Almost all women in Phillippines terminate breast-feeding as soon as they believe that they are pregnant again, because they beleive that the milk belongs to the new baby (International Nutrition Communication Services, 1983).

Birth Order

The general pattern that emerges from various studies is that the risk of infants is relatively high for first births, decreases second and third births, increases slightly for fourth births, and increases much more sharply for later order births. Such a pattern is frequently described as a J-shaped curve. When risks for first births are very high, the curve becomes a U-shaped curve.

The reasons may be that first births include a disproportionate number of difficult deliveries which may be associated with above average infant mortality. In addition, a disproportionate number of first births occur to women at ages which are well below the physiological optimum for reproduction. At the higher orders, infant mortality rates rise once again, partly reflecting a shorter average spacing between births of high parity women. This is probably associated not only with poorer nutrition for the infants, also perhaps with poorer health among mothers. The highest parity women have on an average inferior living conditions and are less able to provide their children with appropriate medical care and adequate nutrition (Frank Mott, 1982: 14-15).

The Khanna Longitudinal Study conducted in 11 Punjab villages, India, revealed that a relatively higher mortality rates were evident for first births and for higher than seventh order births, the intermediate rates fluctuated that no consistent pattern could be discerned (Wyon, and Gorden, 1962; Gorden, 1969). Similar pattern is observed by another study conducted in Gandhigram, Tamilnadu, India (Omran, A.R., *et al.,* 1976: 207-214).

A study conducted in Lucknow city, India, showed more or less the similar pattern that the incidence of infant mortality is the minimum with second birth order of infants. It is relatively higher for the first birth order, fluctuates at still higher level in third or fourth birth order of infants and rises further for birth order of infants of five and above (Saksena, *et al.,* 1980: 52-53).

A study conducted in Hyderabad city revealed that infants of lower birth order 1-3 are seen to be taller and heavier compare to infants of higher birth order (Visweswara Rao and Gopalan, 1971: 186).

The U.S. National Centre for Health Statistics (1973) reported on a sample of 107, 038 infants of the birth cohort registered in 1960 who died when they were under one year of age, infant risk showed a linear relationship to total birth order. The highest mortality risks were registered for high birth order infants of young mothers (especially teenagers) and are for high birth order infants of older mothers. The best survival chances were those for first infants born to mothers between 20 and 30 years of age, first and second infants born to 25-29 years of age, and third infants born to mothers aged 30 to 34 years.

Birth Spacing

The spacing of pregnancies—the time interval between pregnancies is very important. As mentioned earlier when woman has pregnancies closed together, the risk for the infant increases. There is a chance that the pregnancy will end in miscarriage or an infant born alive will die. Having births too close together does not allow the woman's body to recover from the strain of pregnancy, childbirth and breast-feeding. Further more a short interval between births means that the woman will have to care for several young children at the same time. Children too suffer when they are born close together.

During the past fifty years, a number of studies have produced evidence to show that the age at pregnancy and spacing of births has an effect on the health of the mothers and their children. These studies, however, were mainly carried out in the industrialised countries, where maternal and child deaths were already fairly low. More recent work on the timing and spacing of births is focussed on the developing world.

In 28 developing countries for which world fertility survey data were analysed on an average one third of birth intervals were found to be under two years. Short intervals are more common in Latin America (38%) than in Asia (28%) and are especially widespread in the Middle East. (John Cleland, *et al.*, 1989).

Rutstein looked at the World Fertility Survey data from 29 developing countries on spacing of births. The findings are that there is higher infant, toddler and child mortality after short intervals (under 24 months), than after 'normal' intervals (between 24 and 47 months), and mortality goes down still further among those born after 'long' intervals (48 months or more) (Rutstein shea, 1983: 32-33). Child mortality declines, the birth interval increases (Wimilheff - Beverly, 1983).

The WHO study also revealed similar pattern. Closely spaced births and child bearing during the late and early phases of the reproductive life span, enhance not only the risk of maternal mortality and morbidity, but also the risk of infant and child mortality and morbidity (W.H.O. 1983). Children born after a birth interval of one year or less are two times more likely to die than children born after a birth interval of two or more years. (W.H.O., 1984).

For 39 developing countries the risk that a child will die within the first month of life if born within two years of a surviving sibling is 58 per cent greater than if no previous child has been born in the two year interval; the risk is 96 per cent greater during the balance of the first year of life and decreases thereafter. If the previous child died then the relative risk is generally even greater; 249 per cent in the first month and 194-per cent for the balance of the first year (Anne Pebly, 1986: 71-79).

Data collected by the Pan American Health Organisation have documented an increase in deaths among infants born after short intervals (Omran, *et al.,* 1976; Puffer, *et al.,* 1975). Thus, it is found that the risk of deaths among infants born after short interval is higher. Therefore, there is a realisation in many countries of the need to space births.

Sex Preference in Care

Studies in India and other countries have shown strong son preference and also preference for their health care. In India, by tradition and custom they tend to discriminate against daughters.

Some communities in certain parts of India, particularly, Uttar Pradesh, Punjab, Rajasthan, Jammu and Kashmir as well as parts of Gujarat are known to have killed their daughters at least upto the mid 19th century (O'Malley, 1968: 357). Recently Venkataramani, an investigative journalist has brought to light the practice of female infanticide among Kallars, a community of landless labourers in the Madhurai district of Tamil Nadu (Venkataramani, 1986: 26-33).

A study conducted in two villages of Western Uttar Pradesh and one in Eastern Uttar Pradesh and one in urban centre, Lucknow reveals that sons are preferred for old age support and also to carry over the name of the family for the coming generations (Khan, M.E., *et al.,* 1986: 4-7).

A study in two villages of West Bengal documented a high prevalance of various degrees of malnutrition among girls than boys. It was also observed that 50 per cent of mothers did not mind having any number of sons but disliked having many duaghters. Parents did not consider daughters as perspective earners for the family (Senapati, *et al.,* 1990: 15-19). Miller highlighted that boys in North India tend to get better food and better medical care than girls. (Miller, 1981). Ghosh's data on 'treatment seeking behaviour' in Safdarjung Hospital, New Delhi, revealed that boys were treated earlier while girls received treatment in only severe cases. (Ghosh, 1986: 1). Khan has gathered evidence indicating discrimination against daughters in the duration of breast-feeding, other feeding and medical care (Khan, *et al.,* 1986: 3-20).

A household survey of 151 families was conducted over 8 weeks in a squatter settlement within the city limits of Lahore (Pakistan). The mean duration of breast-feeding was 17 months with a tendency for longer breast-feeding of boys and early introduction of solids for girls. Prevalence rates for various diseases were the same for both boys and girls. More girls than boys were significantly wasted, as well as both stunted and wasted. More girls than boys had died (Sabis, 1984: 237-239).

A study conducted in rural Bangladesh also provides conclusive documentation of higher female than male mortality from shortly after birth through the child bearing ages. In the post-neo-natal period female mortality in Bangladesh exceed that of males by as much as 50 per cent.

Son preference in parental care and feeding patterns, food distribution and treatment of illness favouring male children are possible causes of such aberrant childhood mortality differences by sex (D' Souza, Stan, and Ctan, 1980: 257-270).

A group of 598 families in low income districts of Cairo was randomly chosen to receive regular monthly visits by a team of trained field investigators over a one year period. The study finds no significant sex difference in nutritional status until the 6th month of life. Around this period, two fifths of female group but one fourth of the male show signs of malnutrition as measured by weight. The difference continues to increase and is statistically significant by the end of the year. Nutritional status of female infants tended to decline with an addition of daughters in the family. (Ahmed, *et al.*, 1981: 25-29).

Utilisation of Health Services

Health services play an important role in providing good health for mothers and it is particularly important to ensure better survival of the infant. This depends on proper ante-natal care, post-natal care and regular immunisation. There are no studies available showing the exact relationship between health services and infant health. However, utilisation of health services in this section is reviewed.

The purpose of ante-natal care is to ensure good health in every expectant mother, to enable her to have a normal delivery and a healthy baby and to teach the art of child care. Thus, the ante-natal care is meant not for just detecting of rare abnormalities but also for the supervision of the normal pregnancy.

In rural India, very few women go for medical check-up during their pregnancy. A study conducted by Lakshmamma in Praksam district of Andhra Pradesh revealed that about 21.0 per cent of women have received tetanus injection during their last pregnancy. (Lakshmamma, 1991: 193). Another study conducted by Jorapur in Yalandur P.H.C in Karnataka revealed that 23.4 per cent of pregnant women received iron-folic tablets (Jorapur, 1979: 33). A study conducted in Andhra Pradesh showed that Mother and Child Health Services were inadequate and underutilised. The reasons are long distance of the service delivary units, discourtesy shown by health personnel, non-availability of medicine, long waiting time, lack of relief after treatment, and the demand of money by health personnel for the services provided (Reddy, 1989: 221). Another study conducted in a rural area of Maharastra revealed that only one fourth of the households (3,606) visited Primary Health Centres (P.H.Cs) during the 12 months preceding the study (Ram and Datta, 1978; 135-136). The study also revealed that the utilisation of health services varied according to the distance from PHCs.

In the rural areas of India and Ethiopia, the proportion of mothers who had not received pre-natal care were as high as 56 per cent and 88 per cent respectively. In these two countries, pregnant women were likely to be attended by traditional midwives rather than by any other category of health personnel (W.H.O, 1984.)

The health of the new born baby is closely related to care at birth. It will reduce complications at birth, while factors like prematurity or low birth weight (malnourishment) will reflect pre-natal care factors, neonatal tetanus as well as asyphyxia could be a function of the care at birth.

In most of the developing countries, delivery is conducted by relatives and untrained dais (local attendant), and not by trained dais, nurses or doctors. If proper care is taken at the time of delivery, one can ensure better survival of the infant and good health for the mother. A study conducted in rural area of Kurnool district, Andhra Pradesh, revealed that 92.5 per cent of all births delivered at home. The reasons are convenient (91.5%), hospital far off (6.3%), fear of hospital (1.5%), and others (0.7%). It is a sad fact that after many years of independence, except in Kerala a large majority of rural babies continue to be delivered by untrained 'dais' or relatives (Anrudh Jain, and Pravin Visaria, 1988: 34).

An analysis of the reproductive history of women in Uttar Pradesh revealed that as high as 90 per cent of births were delivered at home and 85-90 per cent of the deliveries were assisted by untrained 'dais' and old ladies from home or neighbourhood. The services of the "ANMs are not keenly sought (Khan, 1986: 12). Another study was undertaken in the same state in the rural areas of three districts: Agra, Mathura, and Gazipur. In these districts, the majority of births were attended by family members and neighbours (63%), about 31 per cent by untrained dais, and only 7 per cent of births were assisted by trained professionals in the year 1982 (Khan, 1988: 27).

The percentage of births attended by trained health personnel in 1984 in India was 33 per cent, Pakistan 24 per cent, Nepal 10 per cent, and Bhutan 3 per cent and Sri Lanka

87 per cent and Singapur 100 per cent (John Ross, Molzan and Pensak, 1988: 37).

Immunisation

Immunisation is to produce in an individual a degree of resistance to infectional diseases. The resistance in an infant can be built up against many of common infectious diseases (diphtheria, purtosis, tetanus, polio, measles, tuberculosis, etc.) by administering the appropriate vaccine. Immunisation is most economical and cost effective of all the health interventions in reducing the incidence of disease. Thus, it is an important component of health services. In general, in India the immunisation status of infants and other children is very low.

A study was conducted in the rural ICDS block Kathura, Haryana. The immunisation status of children (0-6 age) is: B.C.G. 18.2 per cent, DPT 6.7 per cent, polio nil, expectant mothers tetanus toxoide 1.0 per cent. (Sunder Lal., 1980: 293-296).

A baseline survey was conducted in 1981 in the urban ICDS block, Pune, Maharastra. The immunisation status of children (0-6 age) is: B.C.G 61.6 per cent, DPT 52.2 per cent, and Polio 52.7 per cent. (Mahendale, S.M., 1985: 1-7).

A study conducted in thirty clusters of Hassan District, Karnataka revealed that 51 per cent of children (12 to 23 months) have received full package of vaccination, while 44 per cent received one or two doses only and 5 per cent of the children never received any vaccination. Vaccine-wise, the coverage is the highest for B.C.G (86%) followed by DPT (79%), Polio (70%) and measles (63%). More than 90 per cent of the vaccinations are given under the facilities created by the programme. The least users of the programme are children of Scheduled Castes and Muslim families (Rayappa and Johson, 1989: 5-7).

Most of the mothers did not give immunisation to their children due to the lack of knowledge of availability and usefulness of vaccines available and also fear of side effects which are created by unskilled health personnel (U.N. 1985). To take a sick child to a PHC or a sub-centre requires effort and expenditure that is beyond the capacity of many rural households in India (Leela Visaria, 1988: 91).

The goals set for immunisation by the world summit for children held in Sep. 1990 at the United Nations headquarters in New York is 90 per cent coverage of immunisation in every province and, where possible in every district (James P. Grant, 1992: 14).

It is interesting to note that in many developed countries of Western Europe, the health problems were very similar not so long ago and have finally controlled by the development of suitable health programmes. Italy and United States of America have sustained better pre-natal and postnatal care practices, improved medical technology and effective medical supervision. In Sweden, women will always receive special care by specialists even if her subsequent pregnancies are normal. The systematic referral system makes a major contribution to the completeness and uniformity of the Swedish pre-natal care system. Sweden has the standardised and thorough set of services available, and Italy seems to fall somewhere in-between. In Sweden, Hungary and all the economically advantaged groups, most women had received pre-natal care and most mothers had paid more than three visits to pre-natal services (WHO, 1981).

Family Planning

Family Planning is an effective way to avoid high risk pregnancies and to ensure better survival of an infant. It improves the health of the women by enabling them to have a few children. Having a large number of children increases the mother's and children's risk of illness or death. In otherwords, pregnancies endanger maternal and infant health if they are "too young, too old, too many, too close". (Population Reports, 1984). The infants born as a result of high-risk pregnancies are even more vulnerable. With these pregnancies there is greater risk of still birth, or death during pregnancy, of various health problems in infancy. From infancy to adolescence children born into large or closely spaced families experience more sickness, slower growth, lower level of academic achievement (Population Reports, 1984). Family Planning helps in increasing spacing of births. Family Planning Programmes can not guarantee infant health, but by protecting families against high risk pregnancy, family planning saves and reduces illness.

The United Nations Children's Fund (UNICEF) has endorsed family planning as one of the high priority techniques for improving child health, along with growth monitoring, oral rehydration therapy, breast-feeding, immunisation, food supplements, and female education. The whole programme is referred to as GOBI-FPF (Grant 1984: 42).

The impact of family planning on infant mortality can be much greater in developing countries, where a large proportion of pregnancies are high risk. Studies in Costa Rica and Chile show that the decrease in the proportion of births that occur to older women and in large families has already contributed to decline in infant mortality rates (Carvojal, 1979).

Many studies have shown that the risk of having a child with Down's syndrome increases as women grow older. (Hay, 1971: 572-581; Hook, 1976: 33-34; 1978: 223-228). Poor maternal nutrition which may be related to repeated child bearing can damage child nutrition in several ways. It may reduce birth weight thus, placing the infant at greater risk of death or illness (Dunn, 1979: 233-240; Harrison, 1979: 52-59; Petro-Barvasian, 1978: 9-15. Prentice, *et al.,* 1983: 439-492; Whitehead, 1981: 168). In extreme cases it also may reduce the quality and quantity of breast milk on which infant growth depends. (Abbott Laboratories, 1978: 23; Atlah, 1980: 229-235; Belavady, 1979: 264-273; Geissler, *et al.,* 1978: 160-168; Hambreau, 1979: 233-244; Hanafi, *et al.,* 1972: 187-191; Horger, 1977, 257-261; Rajalakshmi, 1979: 184-292; Whichelow, 1975: 669; Wray, 1979: 197-229). Children from large families may suffer from infectious illness more often because their siblings are a major source of infection (Saecd Qureshi, *et al.,* 1981: 164-172; Aaby, *et al.,* 1983: 693-701; Kown, *et al.,* 1975: 217-227; Dingle, *et al.,* 1964: 39-49; Dawglas, *et al.,* 1958: 177). In rural India practice of family planning is very low. Rcasons for not practising family planning: several psychological, cultural and economic explanations have been advanced for the relatively poor acceptance of birth control. One of the reasons is desire for several children in Indian family. The other one is family planning is not being able to meet the demand for family planning services (IIPS, 1986: 429). In Omran's study (1976) for those who disapproved, the main reasons are the desire for more children, husband's disapproval, mother-in-law's objection and fear of harm to maternal health. Religion was also an important reason especially in Muslims. In the study conducted in Maharashtra the main reason for never use of family planning was "no child" followed by 'desire for a son', 'desire for a daughter' and family planning methods are harmful to health (IIPS, 1986: 429).

Health Education

Poor health education and poverty are the most important causes of malnutrition among infants. Each day 40,000 children die throughout the world. Most of them are in developing countries. Why such difference between the infant mortality rate of 7 per 1000 live births in Sweden and 208 per 1000 live births in Upper Volte. Berthet noted that in the past, three mistakes were made which must not be repeated. The first was not improving the living conditions of the population. The green revolution in India provides a striking example of an important progress which only benefited the wealtheir farmers. A second mistake was to believe that only a medical approach reduces infant mortality. A third error was to overlook the importance of health education and not to seek active participation of the people concerned (Berthet, 1984: 41-49). Nutrition Foundation of India, recommended that through health education, promote exclusive breast-feeding upto to 6 months of age, at which point supplements such as fresh milk and local foods can be introduced, and also educate mothers regarding infant care during infection.

A study conducted in two villages of Western Uttar Pradesh and one in Eastern Uttar Pradesh revealed that most of the informants were ignorant of the needs and sources of pre-natal and post-natal precautions such as vaccination, protection against nutritional anaemia through iron and vitamin tablets, etc. (Khan, 1986: 12). This also has to be taken care of through health education.

Illness Episode

Frequency of infant illness is high in India. A much greater proportion of illness is due to preventable diseases borne by food, water, and facies, and also due to bad environmental sanitation. In this section, we will review the illness episode of infants.

A study was conducted in the urban slums of ICDS block, Vijayawada, Krishna district, Andhra Pradesh. Among children of 0-3 age group it was observed that 20.8 per cent did not suffer from any illness, 14.6 per cent suffered from one episode of illness, 17 per cent from two, 19.8 per cent from three and 27 per cent from more than three episodes of the same or different illness. The same study also revealed that the major causes of morbidity among the infants were diarrhoea (28.8%), respiratory infection (19.4%), pyrexia (20.0%), and minor infections and injuries (24.7%) and these were contributing to 92.9 per cent of illness. The average spell of sickness was 2.2 per cent. (Subramanyam, G., *et al.*, 1985: 11-19). The reference period is not specified.

Infants in India on an average suffer about 10.2 illness episodes, which keeps them sick for 51 days in a year and the burden of morbidity in rural area is very high (Walia, 1979).

Frequency of morbidity has been estimated in India. It is about 3.4 sickness per child per year. The sickness rate gradually decreases after one to two years of age and a sharp fall after five years of age. The most common illness which retarded the normal growth of Indian infants are infections of gastro-intestinal tract, respiratory tract, skin infection and other infectious diseases (Indira Kapoor, 1979: 11-12).

Morbidity pattern during first year of life is studied among randomly selected infants born in a hospital, Aligarh, Uttar Pradesh, and also infants in a village nearby. The incidence of respiratory infection was 60 per cent, diarrhoea 46 per cent, vitamin A deficiency 11 per cent, severe anaemia 10 per cent, and otitis 8 per cent. Infants morbidity increased after six months old (Jaiswal, *et al.*, 1981: 735-741).

Another study was conducted in urban health centre, Chetla, Delhi. About 156 infants were studied from birth to 18 months. Illness was defined as an illness of the child for which mothers sought medical aid. The study reveals that there were on an average 25.67 episodes of illness from birth to 18 months. The first three diseases according to risk order were upper respiratory infection diarrhoea and skin disease (Mukerjee, 1979: 17-23)

In a study conducted in the rural ICDS block, Kathura in Haryana revealed that among infants' female morbidity is more than male morbidity. (Sunder Lal, 1985: 23-28). The single most illness that occurs to infants is diarrhoea and is especially common in infants born underweight. Repeated diarrhoea attacks interfere with the absorption and use of nutrition by the body resulting slow growth contributing to malnutrition, and provoke further infection and disease. It escalates during the weaning period after the age of six months. As food supplements to breast-feeding become necessary exposure to unsterilised foods and containers is inevitable and infant is increasingly exposed. (Erik Eekholm, and Frank Record., 1976: 17).

In Gambia, diarrheoal episodes had a mean duration of three days in children less than 6 months and 4 days after that age. Children below 6 months of age, 40 to 75 per cent of infants suffered from diarrhoea in any 2 month period and the figures rose to 40 to 100 per cent (during the rainy season) at older ages (Rowland, 1983: 87-98).

The findings of the study conducted in Matlab village, Comilla district, Bangladesh showed that on an average there were 3.2 attacks of diarrhoea per child per year and the average duration was 15.9 days per child per year during the first 2 years. (Khan, 1984: 113-119).

Infant Mortality

Infant mortality rate is regarded as one of the most powerful indicators of health and quality of life in a country. An exceptionally high infant mortality rate exceeding 100 per 1000 live births persists in many developing countries including certain parts in India. In sharp contrast to this the rate in many developed countries is below 20 per 1000 live births. It is argued that reductions in infant mortality rate must await on advancement in overall development. However, the success in Srilanka, Costa Rica, China and Cuba bring home the point that it is possible to reduce infant mortality rate substantially without awaiting overall development.

In confirmity with recommendations of WHO and recognising the importance of reduction in infant mortality rate, the Government of India has recommended reduction in IMR to 60 by 2000 AD for the country as a whole. The accomplishment of reduction of IMR of this magnitude is a major challenge facing the health care providers of this country.

For the first time in the country the infant and child mortality survey was conducted by the office of the Registrar General, India in 1979 with financial assistance from the UNICEF. The survey was carried out in the units of the sample Registration System covering around 7.3 lakh households in all the states and Union Territories of the country. Information on births and infant deaths was collected for each of the calendar period 1973 to 1978. In the case of child deaths data were collected for children born during 1973 onwards (Holla, 1985: 105-126). The findings are:

1. The infant and also the child mortality differ widely among various states from around 40 in Kerala to more than 160 in Uttar Pradesh;
2. There is a declining trend, however, in regard to infant and child mortality since 1978;
3. Infant mortality rate is less in urban area compared to rural area as could be expected;
4. In general, the neo-natal mortality exceeds the post neo-natal mortality and in the rural areas it is nearly double than that in urban areas. The absence of proper medical care especially in the ante-natal period to the expectant mothers and the inadequate maternal and child health services in the rural areas might be the contributary factors for high neo-natal mortality;

5. The infant mortality increases with increase in parity and is independent of the level of education of women and their age at marriage;
6. A large number of infant deaths are not medically attended to. Among infants 58 per cent of the deaths were not attended by trained medical practitioners;
7. In the rural areas among infants the major cause of death is tetanus (14. per cent of the total infant deaths) followed by prematurity.

In urban areas among infants, the major cause of death is pre-maturity followed by tetanus. Other causes of infant mortality and child mortality are diarrhoea, gastro-enteritis, dysentery, respiratory illness, and fibrile illness. (Holla, 1985: 105-126).

In India, neo-natal mortality is more than post-neo-natal mortality. Survival in the neo-natal period (1st to 28 days of life) is very much dependent on the condition of the infant at birth, and the major causes of death in the first week of life are prematurity, inter-uterine asyphixia, birth-trauma, congenital anamalies (endogeneous causes) and tetanus neo-natureum. The deaths in the post-neo-natal period are largely due to environmental factors (exogeneous causes) usually infectious diseases, respiratory diseases and malaria (Sengupta, 1971: 46; Kielman, *et al.,* 1983: 172-214; Sunderlal, 1985: 23-28). Among the most important factors affecting child survival in the first year of life are low birth weight, pre-maturity, and supplementary feeding practices.

It is often postulated that as the IMR declines deaths due to exogenous causes are prevented, eliminated and the endogenous causes assume relatively greater importance. Therefore, post-neo-natal mortality is expected to decline more sharply as a result the share of neo-natal mortality in the total deaths would increase with a decrease in the IMR (Leela Visaria, 1988: 67).

On the basis of various symptoms at the time of death of the infant reported by the parents to the interviewer in

Madurai district of Tamilnadu, the probable cause of death is determined. About 36 per cent of the neo-natal deaths are to tetanus, 16 per cent to diarrhoea and other gastro-intestinal causes, and other 13 per cent to obstetric causes. Nearly one eighth of the post-neo-natal deaths are also attributed to diarrhoea and 12 per cent to other gastro-intestinal causes (Gunasekharan, 1988: 251).

According to Registrar General of India, causes of infant mortality in rural India for the year 1988 comprises mainly conditions of prematurity (45.8%), respiratory infection of new born (17.2%), congenital malformation (3.2%) and birth injury (1.4.%) (Registrar General of India, 1990).

The causes of death under one year of age occuring in a sample of 23 thousand infants born in 8 United States cities in 1911-1916 is analysed. The infant mortality rate was 111.2 per 1000 live births. One third of these deaths were due to birth injuries, prematurity, and congenital defects (Woodbury, 1925).

About age of the mother, the higher mortality risk is found for infants born to every young and very old mothers. In general, this factor show a U-or-J-shaped relationship with infant mortality, *i.e.*, the infant mortality rate is found to be highest at the very young and old ages of child bearing and lower in the middle ages (20-39 years) (Population Reports, 1984; Mahapatra, 1984: 643-649; Kanitkar and Murthy, 1988: 304-305).

Talwar found that the risk of infant mortality among children born to women aged either less than 20 or 40 or more years in rural Madhya Pradesh is 34 per cent higher than that among children born to women between 20 and 39 years of age. (Talwar, 1988: 328).

About birth order or parity, similar relationship is found with infant mortality. Infant mortality is high for first order birth, declines slowly upto the third birth order and then again takes an upward turn. The available literature provides enough evidence that IMR is associated with birth order (Khan, 1988: 233). Another factor that confounds the effect of age and parity or birth order on infant mortality is the length of the preceding birth interval. Data from both developed and developing countries suggest that birth interval is a major determinant of infant mortality. The shorter the birth interval, the higher are the chances of infant deaths (Gandotra, *et al.*, 1982; Swensen, 1977: 1-16 Wolfers and Scrimsaw, 1975: 479-76; Wyon and Gordan, 1962: 17-32; Yerushalmy, *et al.*, 1956: 80-96).

Studies indicate that infant mortality is much higher when the mother is illiterate, marries young or does not have trained birth attendants, place of delivery and household environment such as water sanitation, and housing condition. Studies also indicate that literacy, age at marriage, and trained assistance at birth are linked to the class and caste of the mother (Meera Chatterjee, 1985: 224-240).

2

SOCIO-ECONOMIC AND DEMOGRAPHIC BACKGROUND OF THE RESPONDENTS

Introduction

The economic and social inequality in the context of infant health has been an important unsolved problem in India. It is thus important to reduce, or if possible, eliminate the differentials in infant health with regard to different socio-economic groups. In order to achieve this goal, it is necessary to understand socio-economic and demographic differentials among the population. Therefore, the socio-economic background of the study area and that of respondents, (mothers) such as housing conditions, household size, occupations, annual family income, education of husbands and wives, family type, age at marriage, bathing per week, present age of the respondents, number of deliveries, number of live births and number of living children, etc., are discussed in this chapter.

According to 1981 census, in Kuppam Taluq there are 195 villages. The proportion of literates in this taluq is very low (17.98%) compared to Andhra Pradesh as a whole (29.94%). In the rural area, only 14.5 per cent are literates (males 28.9%, females 5.9%, as against 23.24 per cent in the state (males 32.28%, females 14.08%) (Registrar General and Census Commissioner of India, 1983: 41).

In this taluq, electricity is supplied to only 54.3 per cent of the total villages. The availability of cultivable land to total is 38.8 per cent and the percentage of irrigated land to total cultivable land is 15.5 per cent only. (Director of Census Operations, A.P., 1986: 62).

Housing Conditions

Housing is one of the basic needs of mankind. The quality of housing is determined by material used for construction of walls and roofs.

In the study area, out of 505 respondents, majority of the respondents are living in 'Huts' (42.6%), and 38.6 per cent of the respondents are living in 'Katcha' houses. The remaining proportion of 18.8 per cent of the respondents are living in 'Pucca' houses. Kuppam taluq belongs to a backward area and hence, the housing conditions are very poor. Walls of mud and roofs of thatch (grass) are predominant in the study area.

Community

Religion and caste groups probably reflect the socio-economic differences rather than innate differences among the groups themseleves. In Andhra Pradesh as in other parts of the country, villages are formed with certain caste groups. In the study area the Forward Community constitutes 20.0 per cent, Backward Community 36.0 per cent, Scheduled Castes and Scheduled Tribes 15.4 and 15.2 per cent respectively. Muslims constitute 13.3 per cent. Backward Community constitutes the major group in the study area.

In the study area, the castes that belong to Forward Community are Reddy, Brahmin, Balija, Vysya, Modaliar, Kamma and Kapu. Backward Community Constitute many castes—Kummara, Jangama, Washermen, Palli, Mangali, Vanne Kapu, Weavers, Dharmaraju Kapu, Valmiki, Gowdas, Kurapa, Besta, Boya, Kamsala, Doodekula, and Gandla. Scheduled Castes constitute Mala and Madiga, Scheduled Tribe constitute Sugalis only, Muslims constitute Shaik, Sayyed and Patans.

Household Size

Persons living in a house with a common kitchen is defined as 'household'. The total number of persons living in a house with a common kitchen is measured as household size. In the study area, the range of the household size is 3 to 35 members. The average size of a household is 7.6 persons and its standard deviation is 4.58. The majority of the respondents are from the household size of 6 to 10 members (52.1%). The next highest proportion (33.7%) is from the household size of 3 to 5 members. Only about 14.3 per cent of the households have more than 10 members. From table 2.1, it is observed that large household is predominant in the Forward Communities.

Among the different communities, the average size of the household is highest in the Forward Community (9.5), followed by Muslims (7.7), Backward Community (7.1), Scheduled Tribe (6.6) and Scheduled Caste (6.4) as shown in Table 2.1.

Table 2.1. Number and Percentage Distribution of Respondents by Household Size and Community

Community	*Household size*				
	3-5	*6-10*	*11 +*	*Total*	*Average*
Forward Community	38 (27.7)	49 (48.5)	24 (23.8)	101 (100.0)	9.5
Backward Community	52 (28.6)	107 (58.8)	23 (12.6)	182 (100.0)	7.1
Scheduled Caste	37 (47.4)	34 (43.6)	7 (9.0)	78 (100.0)	6.4
Scheduled Tribe	33 (42.8)	36 (46.8)	8 (10.4)	77 (100.0)	6.6
Muslims	20 (29.0)	37 (55.1)	10 (14.9)	67 (100.0)	7.7
Total	**170 (33.7)**	**263 (52.1)**	**72 (14.2)**	**505 (100.0)**	**7.6**

Note: Figures in the parentheses are in percentages.

Occupation of Husbands

In this study, six types of occupations have been classified for husbands and they are cultivators, agricultural labourers, cultivators cum labourers, artisans service and business. In the study area, among the husbands of the respondents, the highest proportion belongs to agricultural labourers (60.1%) followed by cultivators (21.0%), cultivators cum agricultural labourers (11.6%), services and business each 3.0 per cent, and artisans (washermen and pot makers, 1.3%). As one would expect the proportion of agricultural labourers is highest among Scheduled

Table 2.2. Number and Percentage Distribution of Respondents by Husband's Occupation and Community

	Agricultural Occupation						
Community	*Cultivators*	*Labourers*	*Cultivators cum labourers*	*Artisans*	*Service*	*Business*	*Total*
Forward Community	52 (52.5)	28 (28.3)	3 (3.0)	—	9 (9.1)	7 (7.1)	99 (100.0)
Backward Community	38 (21.1)	89 (49.4)	40 (22.2)	6 (3.3)	5 (2.8)	2 (1.1)	180 (100.0)
Scheduled Caste	5 (6.4)	68 (87.2)	5 (6.4)	—	—	—	78 (100.0)
Scheduled Tribe	—	76 (98.7)	1 (1.3)	—	—	—	77 (100.0)
Muslims	10 (14.9)	40 (59.7)	9 (13.4)	1 (1.5)	1 (1.5)	6 (9.0)	67 (100.0)
Total	**105** **(21.0)**	**301** **(60.1)**	**58** **(11.6)**	**7** **(1.3)**	**15** **(3.0)**	**15** **(3.0)**	**501*** **(100.0)**

Note: Figures in the parentheses are in percentages.
* For living husbands only.

Tribes. Actually almost all of them are agricultural labourers. They are followed by Scheduled Caste (87%), Muslims (59.7%), Backward Community (49.4%) and Forward Community (28.3%). Within the Forward Community, cultivators are the highest (52.5%). Very few are in services and business and it is nil among Scheduled Castes and Scheduled Tribes (Table 2.2).

Occupation of Respondents

About the respondent's occupation, it is being classified into two groups only, *i.e.*, non-worker (housewife) and worker (agricultural labourers and also artisans), as there are no respondents engaged in any other occupation. There are only three artisans. As high as 75 per cent of the respondents are agricultural labourers and 24.6 per cent are housewives. In the Forward Community 49.5 per cent of the respondents are housewives. In Scheduled Tribe hundred per cent of the respondents and in Scheduled Caste 96.2 per cent of the respondents are labourers, followed by Backward Community (73.6%), Muslims (60.3%), and Forward Community (50.5%) (Table 2.3). Two things are distinctly observed. One, work participation among respondents is very high. Two, even among Forward Community the proportion of workers is high.

Table 2.3 Number and Percentage Distribution of Respondents by Occupation

Religion and Caste	*Occupation*		
	Non-worker	*Worker*	*Total*
Forward Caste	50 (49.5)	51 (50.5)	101 (100.0)
Backward Caste	45 (24.8)	137 (75.2)	182 (100.0)
Scheduled Caste	3 (3.8)	75 (96.2)	78 (100.0)
Scheduled Tribe	—	77 (100.0)	77 (100.0)
Muslims	26 (38.2)	41 (60.3)	67 (100.0)
Total	**124** **(24.6)**	**381** **(75.4)**	**505** **(100.0)**

Note: Figures in the parentheses are in percentages.

Income

The potential role of income in infant health is complex due to multifactor nature of income itself. Data both on income and expenditure of a household are collected. Usually the respondents when they give information on income under-report it and in case of consumption over report it. So to balance these errors and to estimate the correct income, average of income and expenditure is taken as income, and this income is coded for analysis. In the present study, income is devided into five groups according to their annual income. Income group is categorised into very low income, low income, middle income, and better income groups.

From Table 2.4, (*See on next page*) one can read that 19 per cent of the respondents is belonging to 'very low income' (those families whose annual income is less than Rs. 2000). The highest proportion of the respondents (62.0%) belong to 'low income' group (Rs. 2001 to 4000). About 11.1 per cent belong to 'middle income' group (Rs. 4001 to 6000) and the remaining 7.9 per cent belong to slightly 'better income' group (more than six thousand rupees). Thus, most of the families belong to low and very low income families (less than Rs. 4.000). Among different communities, Scheduled Castes, Scheduled Tribes and Muslims have less income compared to Backward Community and Forward Community families. The average annual family income is Rs. 2,188 in the study sample with a standard deviation of Rs. 1,196.

Education

Education plays an important role in improving the socio-economic conditions of the people especially that of health. In this study, only two categories of literacy level are considered: Literates and Illiterates. In the study area, most of the families belong to illiterates. Education among the respondents and their husbands is very low in the study area. Among husbands 20.0 per cent, and among wives 9.1 per cent are literate. If we analyse in terms of couple as a unit, then only eight per cent of both the husbands and wives are literates. Twelve per cent of literate husbands have illiterate wives, and only 1.2 per cent

Table 2.4 Number and Percentage Distribution of Respondents According to their Family Income and Community

Level of Income (in rupees)	*Comunity*					*Total*
	Forward Caste	*Backward Caste*	*Scheduled Caste*	*Scheduled Tribe*	*Muslims*	
2000	13 (12.9)	33 (18.1)	30 (38.5)	2 (2.6)	18 (26.9)	96 (19.0)
2001—4000	51 (50.5)	109 (59.9)	44 (56.4)	65 (84.4)	44 (65.7)	313 62.0)
4001—6000	7 (16.8)	12 (13.2)	— (5.1)	1 (10.4)	1 (4.5)	56 (11.1)
6000—8000	7 (6.9)	12 (6.6)	—	1 (1.3)	1 (1.5)	21 (4.2)
8001—10000	2 (2.0)	3 (1.6)	—	—	—	5 (1.0)
10000+	11 (10.9)	1 (0.5)	—	1 (1.3)	1 (1.5)	5 (2.7)
Total	**101** **(100.0)**	**182** **(100.0)**	**78** **(100.0)**	**77** **(100.0)**	**67** **(100.0)**	**505** **(100.0)**

Note: Figures in the parentheses are in percentages.

of illiterate husbands have literate wives; 78.8 per cent of both the husbands and wives are illiterates. The association between husband's literacy and wife's literacy is statistically significant at 1% level of probability ($X^2 = 141.8$, $p = 0.01$ for 1 d.f.).

Table 2.5 Number and Percentage Distribution of Husband's and Wives by Literacy Level

Husband's literacy	*Wife's literacy*		
	Literate	*Illiterate*	*Total*
Literate	40 (7.9)	61 (12.1)	101 (20.0)
Illiterate	6 (1.2)	398 (78.8)	404 (80.0)
Total	**46** **(9.1)**	**459** **(90.9)**	**505** **(100.0)**

Note: Figures in the parentheses are in percentages.

Habits According to Occupation of Husbands and Wives

Husbands

A good amount of family income is spent on some of the addictions namely, smoking, drinking, chewing tobbacco, and playing cards. The money spent on these addictions if utilised for food and health, then the health status of children can be improved a lot. So these habits are enquired in the survey. Among husbands, 59.0 per cent are smokers. The highest proportion of smokers are found to be among business community (86.7%) followed by artisans (71.4%), labourers (63.9%), cultivators cum agricultural labourers (51.7%). The least proportion of smokers is found among service community (33.3%) and cultivators (47.6%). In the study area, about 16 per cent are addicted to drinking alcohol/arrack. It is highest among labourers (24.9%) and in all other communities it is very low. About 26.3 per cent are chewing tobbacco, and it is highest among cultivators cum agricultural labourers (34.5%) followed by labourers (27.2%), and cultivators (25.7%) (Table 2.6).

Table 2.6 Husband's Occupation and His Habits

Husbands Occupation	*Total Husbands*	*Habits*			
		Smoking	*Drinking*	*Playing Cards*	*Chewing Tobbacco*
Cultivators	105	50 (47.6)	2 (1.9)	3 (2.9)	27 (25.7)
Cultivators cum Agri. labourers	58	30 (51.7)	2 (3.4)	3 (5.2)	20 34.5)
Labourers	305	195 (63.7)	76 (24.9)	26 (8.5)	83 (27.2)
Artisans	7	5	—	—	1 (14.3)
Service	15	5 (33.3)	—	—	1 (6.7)
Business	15	13 (86.7)	1 (6.7)	2 (13.3)	1 (6.7)
Total	**505 (100.0)**	**298 (59.0)**	**81 (16.0)**	**34 (6.7)**	**133 (26.3)**

Note: Figures in the parentheses are in percentages.

Wives

Among wives, only 3 per cent are smokers. About 11.0 per cent of wives consume alcohol/arrack; and these wives are taking only at the time of festivals and it is found to be highest among labourers (14.3%) particularly among Scheduled Tribe labourers. About half of the women are chewing tobbacco and this also is found to be highest among labourers (54.2%). Children's health and mother's health will be better if the money spent on these habits is spent on nutritious food (*See table 2.7*)

Family Type

Nuclear family is defined as a family with father, mother and their unmarried children. All other families are categorised as joint families. As time passing,family formation is changing. In this study area, majority of the families are of joint family type because of agrarian society. From Table 2.8 one can observe that about 42 per cent of the respondents are from nuclear family and 58 per cent of respondents are from joint family. If

Table 2.7 Wife's Occupation and Her Habits

Wife's Occupation	*Total Wives*	*Habits*		
		Smoling	*Drinking*	*Chewing Tobbacco*
Housewife	124	2 (1.6)	1 (0.8)	43 (34.7)
Labourer	378	13 (3.4)	54 (14.3)	205 (54.2)
Artisan	3	—	—	1 (33.3)
Total	**505**	**15** **(3.0)**	**55** **(10.9)**	**249** **(49.3)**

Note: Figures in the parentheses are in percentages

Table 2.8 Number and Percentage Distribution of Respondents of Type of Family and Community

Community	*Type of family*		
	Nuclear	*Joint*	*Total*
Forward Community	33 (32.7)	38 (67.3)	101 (100.0)
Backward Community	77 (42.3)	105 (57.7)	182 (100.0)
Scheduled Caste	33 (42.3)	45 (57.7)	78 (100.0)
Scheduled Tribe	36 (46.8)	41 (53.2)	77 (100.0)
Muslims	34 (50.7)	33 (49.3)	67 (100.0)
Total	**213** **(42.2)**	**292** **(57.8)**	**505** **(100.0)**

Note: Figures in the parentheses are in percentages.

we look the families community-wise, the joint family system is prevailing more among Forward Community (67.3%), followed by Backward Community and Scheduled Caste (57.7% each). Among Scheduled Tribes, the proportion is 53.2 per cent.

But among Muslims, only 43.3 per cent of the respondents are in joint family. Thus, the study reveals that the joint family system is popular among Forward Community, compared to Backward Community, Scheduled Caste and Scheduled Tribe, and it is least in Muslim Community.

Bathing

Since regular bath is one of the parameters of personal hygiene, information on frequency of bath is collected in this study. It is observed that very high proportion (64.4%) of the respondents are used to take bath only once in a week. About 21 per cent are taking bath twice in a week. Only 10 per cent are used to take bath three times and above per week (*i.e.*, alternative days) and 4.7 per cent stated that they do not take bath even once in a week (Table 2.9). If we analyse bathing by

Table 2.9 Number and Percentage Distribution of Respondents by Bath per Week

Community	*Bath per week*				
	0	*1*	*2*	*3 & above*	*Total*
Forward Caste	3 (2.9)	51 (50.5)	23 (22.8)	24 (23.8)	101 (100.0)
Backward Caste	7 (3.8)	140 (76.9)	26 (14.3)	9 (5.0)	182 (100.0)
Scheduled Caste	7 (9.0)	58 (74.4)	12 (15.4)	1 (1.2)	78 (100.0)
Scheduled Tribe	5 (6.5)	42 (54.5)	18 (23.4)	12 (15.6)	77 (100.0)
Muslims	2 (3.0)	34 (50.7)	27 (40.3)	4 (6.0)	67 (100.0)
Total	**24** **(4.7)**	**325** **(64.4)**	**106** **(21.0)**	**50** **(9.9)**	**505** **(100.0)**

Note: Figures in the parentheses are in percentages

community, higher proportion of respondents of the Forward Community are taking three times or more per week, than the other communities. For the total sample, on an average the respondents use to take bath 1.54 times per week with a standard deviation of 1.31. In spite of availability of water, the frequency of bathing is very low. In fact, they are habituated to take bath once in a week and do not know the benefits of bath (healthy, active and freshness). But infants are given bath every day.

Age Distribution

The age distribution of the respondents is given in the table 2.10. The number of respondents is highest in the age group of 20-24 (37.8%) followed by 25-29 (27.3%). In all other groups, it is less than 15 per cent. Respondents are categorised into three categories: young (less than or equal to 29 years), middle (30-39 years) and old women (40 and over). Eighty per cent of the respondents are young and 18.2 per cent belong to middle age group. The remaining 1.8 per cent are old women. There are considerable proportion (14.9%) of very young women (15-19 age group). For better health of children further reduction of women with an infant child in the age group of 15-19 is very essential.

Table 2.10 Age Distribution of the Respondents

Age of the respondents	*Number of women*	*Percentage*	*Cumulative percentage*
15—19	75	14.9	14.9
20—24	191	37.8	52.7
25—29	138	27.3	80.0
30—34	62	12.3	92.3
35—39	30	5.9	98.2
40—44	8	1.6	99.8
45—49	1	0.2	100.0
Total	**505**	**100.0**	

Age at Marriage

Age at mariage is an important parameter of bearing children. It depends on socio-economic and cultural conditions of a society. In the study area, the highest proportion of the respondents (55.4 %) got married between the age of 11 to 15 years and 5.7 per cent of respondents got married at 10 years of age or below (Table 2.11). Thus, majority of women are

Table 2.11 Number and Percentage Distribution of Respondents according to their Age at Marriage and Community

Community	*Age at Marriage*					
	19 Yrs.	*11-15 Yrs.*	*16-17 Yrs.*	*18+ Yrs.*	*Total*	*Mean Age at Marriage*
Forward Caste	2 (2.0)	42 (41.6)	24 (23.8)	33 (32.7)	101 (100.0)	15.73
Backward Caste	15 (8.2)	110 (60.4)	29 (15.9)	28 (15.4)	182 (100.0)	14.23
Scheduled Caste	5 (6.4)	47 (60.3)	8 (10.3)	18 (23.1)	78 (100.0)	14.55
Scheduled Tribe	5 (6.4)	39 (50.6)	11 (14.3)	22 (28.6)	77 (100.0)	15.02
Muslims	2 (3.0)	42 (62.7)	11 (16.4)	12 (17.9)	67 (100.0)	14.56
Total	**29** **(5.7)**	**280** **(55.4)**	**83** **(16.4)**	**113** **(22.5)**	**505** **(100.0)**	**14.75**

Note: Figures in the parentheses are in percentages.

married at a young age, only 22.5 per cent of women got married at age 18 years and above.

If we analyse age at marriage by community-wise, the highest proportion of the Forward Community respondents (32.7%) got married at age 18 years and above followed by Scheduled Tribes (28.6%), Scheduled Castes (23.1%), Muslims (17.9%) and Backward Community (15.4%). There are considerable number of respondents who married at 10 years of age and below in all communities. The mean age at marriage in the study area is 14.75 years, with a standard deviation of 3.14 years. The highest mean age at marriage is observed in Forward Community (15.73 years) and the lowest is observed in Backward Community (14.23 years).

Number of Deliveries, Live-births and Living Children

Average number of deliveries, live-births or living children is an important index of fertility, which depends on the socio-economic, cultural and demographic background of the couples. In the study area, about 24.8 per cent of the respondents have one living child, 27.9 per cent have two children, 20.8 per cent are with three children, 14.9 per cent are with four children, 5.7 per cent are with five children, and 5.9 per cent are with six and above living children at the time of survey (Table 2.12). The average number of deliveries (live-births plus still births) per woman observed is 3.37. Child health is expected to be improved if family planning methods are practised after two children and there are about 47 per cent who have more than two children. The average number of live births and living children are 3.21 and 2.72 per woman respectively. Thus the loss of children after live-birth is 0.49 per woman. It means that approximately there is a loss of one child for every two women. This indicates a heavy loss of children and low child health. The loss of children is more in certain age groups. The difference between average number of deliveries and average number of live-births is more after age 35 and the difference between average number of live-births and average number of living children is more after age 30. It does mean that the loss of children is more after age 30 in the study area (Table 2.12 and Fig. 2.1)

Table 2.12 Average Number of Deliveries, Live-births and Living Children of the Respondents According to Their Age

Age of the Respondents	*No. of women*	*Average no. of Deliveries*	*Average no. of Live-births*	*Average no. of Living Children*	*Difference of 3 and 4 (still births)*	*Difference of 4 and 5 (dead)*
15—19	75	1.41	1.40	1.32	0.01	0.08
20—24	191	2.54	2.42	2.13	0.12	0.29
25—29	138	3.75	3.75	3.12	0.04	0.63
30—34	62	5.34	5.15	4.02	0.19	1.13
35—39	30	6.37	5.53	4.73	0.84	0.80
40—44	8	6.88	5.75	4.88	1.13	0.87
45—49	1	9.00	6.00	6.00	3.00	0.00
Total	**505**	**3.37**	**3.21**	**2.72**	**0.16**	**0.49**

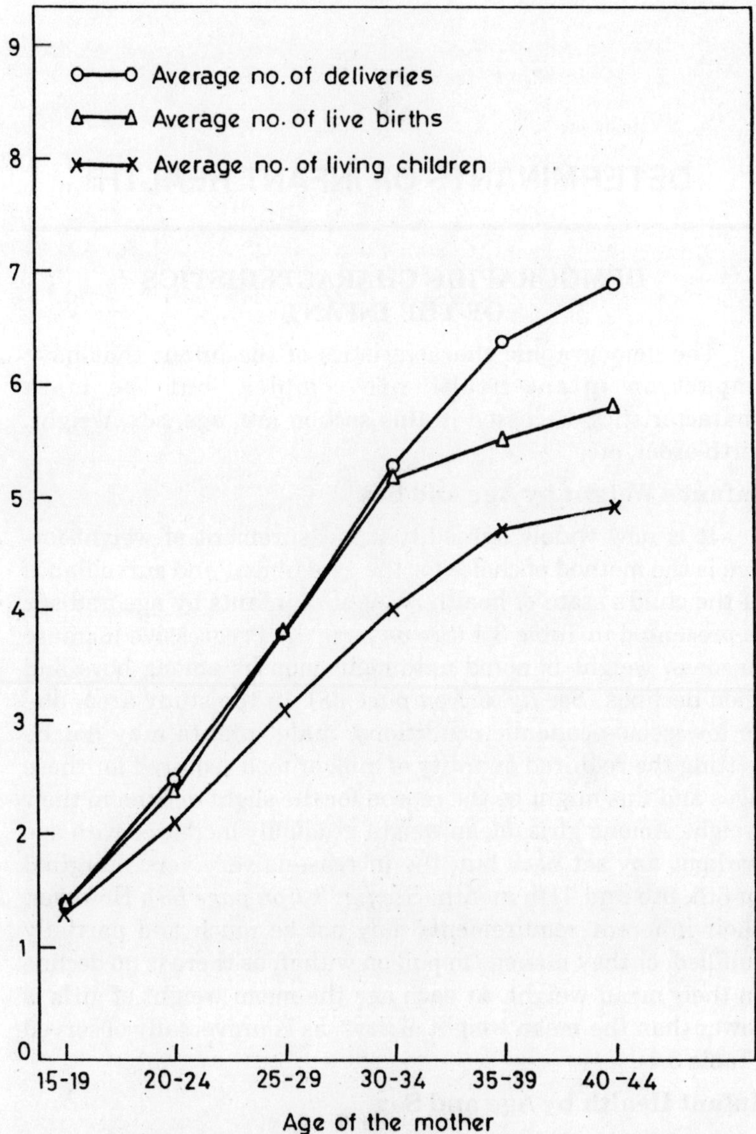

Fig. 2.1. Average Number of Deliveries, Live-births and Living Children of the Respondents According to Their Age

3

DETERMINANTS OF INFANT HEALTH

DEMOGRAPHIC CHARACTERISTICS OF THE INFANT

The demographic characteristics of the infant that have impact on infant health are complex, but the main characteristics discussed in this section are: age, sex, weight, birth order, etc.

Infant's Weight by Age and Sex

It is now widely agreed that measurement of weight-for-age is the method of choice for the assessment and surveillance of the child's state of health. Weight of infants by age and sex is presented in Table 3.1 (*See on page 67)* Progressive increase in mean weight is noted upto eight months among boys and then declines (*See fig. 3.1 on page 68*). In the study area, due to low socio-economic conditions, male infants may not be getting the required quantity of milk or food required for those ages and this might be the reason for the slight decline in their weight. Among girls, mean weight gradually increases with age without any set back but, the increase is very very marginal in 8th, 9th and 11th month (*See fig. 3.1 on page 68*). However, their inherent requirements may not be much and partially fulfilled, or they manage to pull on with it, as there is no decline in their mean weight. At each age the mean weight of girls is lower than the mean weight of boys, as is universally observed (Table 3.1).

Infant Health by Age and Sex

As explained in the first chapter, a child with a weight equal to or above 80 per cent of the W.H.O reference weight for age is categorised as 'normals,' and a child with a weight between 60 to 79 per cent of the reference weight-for-age is categorised

Table 3.1 Mean Weight of Infants by Age and Sex with W.H.O. Reference Weights for Infants

Age of infant (months)	Boys				Girls			
	Number	Mean weight in kgs.	W.H.O. Reference weight* 80%	W.H.O. Reference weight* 60%	Number	Mean weight in kgs.	W.H.O. Reference weight* 80%	W.H.O. Reference weight* 60%
0	17	3.21	2.6	2.0	9	3.07	2.6	1.9
1	15	3.29	3.4	2.6	8	3.25	3.2	2.4
2	12	3.71	4.2	3.1	10	3.40	3.8	2.8
3	22	4.95	4.8	3.6	23	4.46	4.3	3.2
4	18	5.06	5.3	4.0	11	5.27	4.8	3.6
5	22	5.60	5.8	4.4	20	5.32	5.3	4.0
6	31	5.92	6.3	4.7	37	5.54	5.8	4.3
7	18	6.78	6.7	5.0	22	6.24	6.2	4.6
8	26	6.87	7.0	5.3	18	6.25	6.5	4.9
9	16	6.75	7.3	5.5	25	6.26	6.8	5.1
10	15	6.70	7.6	5.7	24	6.66	7.1	5.4
11	46	6.80	7.9	5.9	40	6.67	7.4	5.5
	258	**5.72**			**247**	**5.65**		

Source: *Margaret Cameron and Yugue Haffevander, 1983: 175

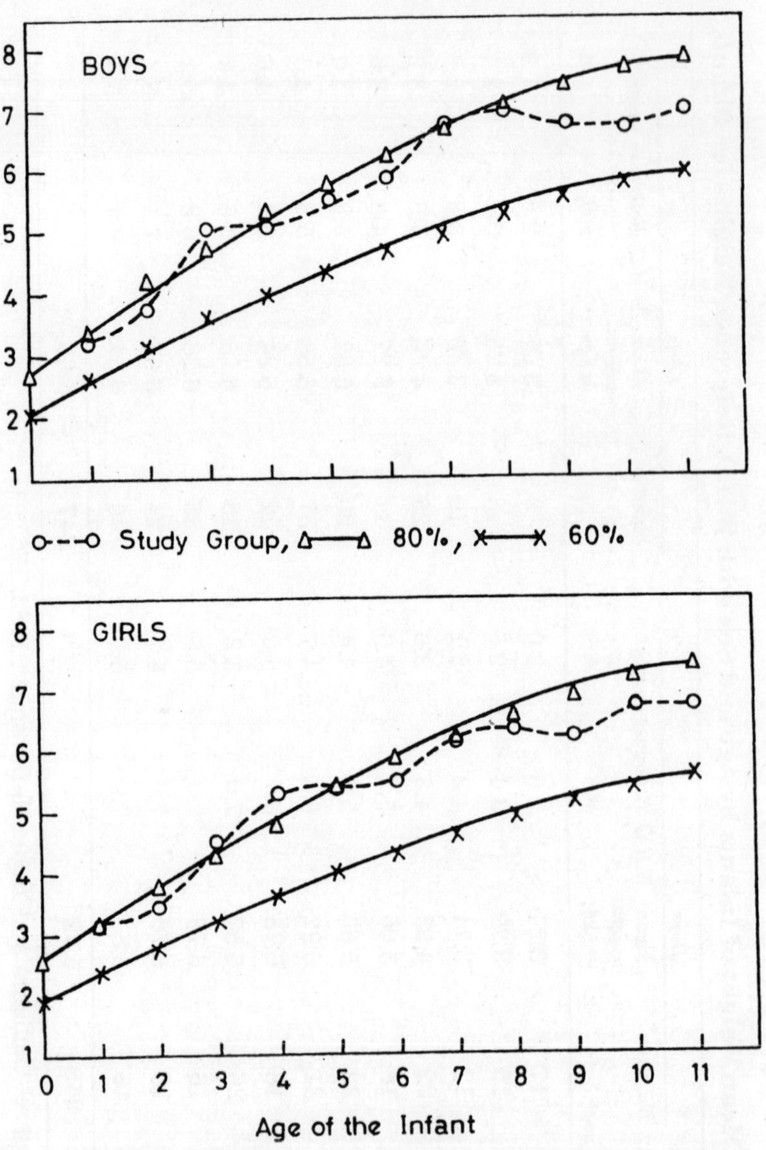

Fig. 3.1 Mean Weight of Infants by Age and Sex with W.H.O. Reference Weights for Infants

as 'poor health,' and a child with a weight below 60 per cent of weight-for-age is categorised as 'very poor health'. Accordingly infant health is examined.

In Table 3.2, infant health is examined by age and sex. In the study area, 44 per cent (male and females together) are of 'normal health' and 43 per cent are of 'poor health' and the remaining 13 per cent are of 'very poor health'. Among boys and girls the proportion of normals are 44.6 per cent and 43.3 per cent respectively and this difference is not statistically significant (Z = 0.29, P> 0.05). The proportion of 'very poor health' in boys and girls is 13.2 per cent and 12.6 per cent respectively showing a marginal difference.

Table 3.2 Number and Percentage Distribution of Infants by Health Status and Sex

Infant	*Boys*	*Girls*	*Total*
Normals	115 (44.6)	107 (43.3)	222 (43.9)
Poor	109 (42.2)	109 (44.1)	218 (43.2)
Very poor	34 (13.2)	31 (12.6)	65 (12.9)
Total	**258** **(100.0)**	**247** **(100.0)**	**505** **(100.0)**

Note: Figures in the parentheses are in percentages

From Table 3.3 it is observed that among boys, the percentage of normals increases from 47.7 per cent in the age group of 0-2 months to 53.3 per cent in 6-8 months, then declines to 29.9 per cent in 9-11 months. Among girls the proportion of the healthy declines continuously from 59.3 per cent in 0-2 months to 28 per cent in the age group of 9-11 months. Thus, the pattern is different between boys and girls. This can be clearly seen in Fig. 3.2. After eight months both among boys and girls there is a steep decline of normals, which again reflects malnutrition among older babies.

Table 3.3 Percentage of Infants of Normal Health by Age and Sex (Percentage to total in each age and for each sex)

Age (months)	*Boys*	*Girls*	*Total*
0—2	21 (47.7)	16 (59.3)	37 (52.1)
3—5	31 (50.0)	28 (51.9)	59 (50.8)
6—8	40 (53.3)	38 (49.4)	78 (51.3)
9—11	23 (29.9)	25 (28.1)	48 (28.3)
Total	**115** **(44.6)**	**107** **(43.3)**	**222** **(43.9)**

Note: Figures in the parentheses are in percentages

Another interesting observation is in the age group 0-2 months, the proportion of healthy children is considerably higher among girls (59%) than boys (48%). This pattern continues in the age group of 3-5 also, though with lesser degree. But on the whole (considering all ages), there is no difference among normals between boys and girls (44.6% and 43.3% respectively), as can be observed from Table 3.3. In developing countries, it is usually assumed that male infants are looked after better than female infants, due to socio-economic and cultural reasons. However, findings of this study do not support this contention. These findings are broadly in confirmity with the study conducted by Lakshmamma (1991, pp. 200) in another part of Andhra Pradesh. She found that majority of the respondents are not giving more importance to sons compared to daughters during normal conditions or also when they are ill.

Birth Order and Infant Health

Birth order has got influence on infant health. Usually infants whose birth order is lower than or equal to three have better health than those whose birth order is higher than three. The assumption is that the care by the mothers will be better if they have fewer children compared to having many children and they themselves would be healthier. In addition to this, it is universally known that there is higher risk for higher birth order children. In this study, among male infants of third or lower order, about 48.7 per cent of infants are healthy, whereas infants whose birth order is more than three, 39.2 per cent of the infants are healthy. (Table 3.4). Thus, among male infants normal infants are more among lower birth order compared to infants of higher birth order. But surprisingly, more female infants of higher birth order (nearly 52%) are healthier than those of lower birth order (37%). As a result of this, a slightly higher proportion of all children (males and females together) of higher birth order (about 47%) is healthier than those of lower birth order (43%).

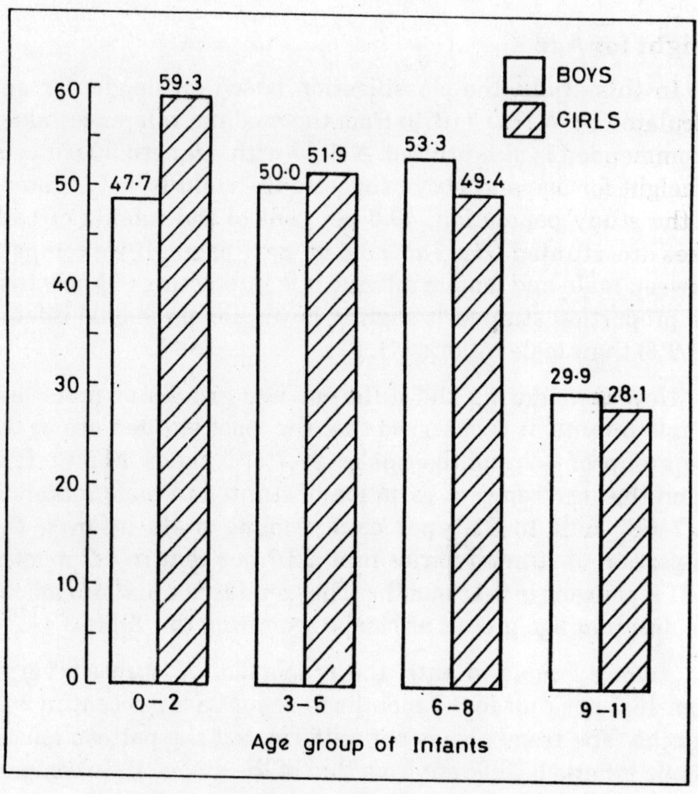

Fig. 3.2 Percentage of Infants of Normal Health by Age and Sex of the Infants

Table 3.4 Proportion of Infants of Normal Health by Birth Order and Sex (Percentage to total for each birth Order and Sex)

Birth Order	*Boys*	*Girls*	*Total*
Less than or equal to 3	76 (48.7)	53 (37.1)	129 (43.1)
More than 3	39 (39.2)	54 (51.9)	94 (45.6)
Total	**115** **(44.6)**	**107** **(43.3)**	**222** **(43.9)**

Note: Figures in the parentheses are in percentages

Height for Age

In this study, the classification based on height for age calculated by W.H.O. (1979) from the medium reference values recommended is also utilised. A child with a length 90 per cent of height for age and above suggests the child is 'not stunted'. In the study population, 40.0 per cent of the infants of both sexes are 'stunted' (*See Table 3.5* on next page). If we compare between male and female infants, it is interesting to know that the proportion stunted is slightly lower among female infants (38.9%) than male infants (41.1%).

Now considering the different age groups of male and female infants, it is observed that the least stunted are in the age group of 0-2 months (males 22.7%; females 18.5%). It is found that the range of variation of stunted in male infants is 22.7 per cent to 51.9 per cent. Among male infants, the proportion of stunted varies from 22.7 per cent in 0-2 months to 51.9 per cent in 9-11 months. The trend is not uniform among the different age groups as can be seen from the Table 3.4.

Among female infants, the proportion of 'stunted' varies from 18.5 per cent in 0-2 months to about 38.2 per cent in 9-11 months. The trend also is not uniform, but the pattern among female infants is different from that of the males. If we compare the classification based on weight-for-age, the majority of infants are of 'not normal' health. But when we considered the height for age the pattern is different. The majority of the

Table 3.5 Age-wise and sex-wise distribution of Infants stunted and not-stunted

	Boys			*Girls*			*Total*		
Age (months)	*Stunted*	*Not Stunted*	*Total*	*Stunted*	*Not Stunted*	*Total*	*Stunted*	*Not Stunted*	*Total*
0-2	10	34	44	5	22	27	15	56	71
	(22.7)	(77.3)	(100.0)	(18.5)	(81.5)	(100.0)	(21.1)	(78.9)	(100.0)
3-5	30	32	62	23	31	54	53	63	116
	(48.4)	(51.6)	(100.0)	(42.6)	(57.4)	(100.0)	(45.7)	(54.3)	(100.0)
6-8	26	49	75	34	43	77	60	92	152
	(34.7)	(65.3)	(100.0)	(44.2)	(55.8)	(100.0)	(39.5)	(60.5)	(100.0)
9-11	40	37	77	34	55	89	74	92	166
	(51.9)	(48.1)	(100.0)	(38.2)	(61.8)	(100.0)	(45.7)	(56.8)	(100.0)
Total	**106**	**152**	**258**	**96**	**151**	**247**	**202**	**303**	**505**
	(41.1)	**(58.1)**	**(100.0)**	**(38.9)**	**(61.1)**	**(100.0)**	**(40.0)**	**(60.0)**	**(100.0)**

Source: Figures in the parantheses are in percentages.

infants are of normal health (stunted). It is an apparent paradox. Nothing'can be said definitely unless we study in detail from all points of view. The possible explanation appears to be that a given set of circumstance might have more adverse effect on weight rather than height.

SOCIO-ECONOMIC BACKGROUND OF MOTHER

Many studies have shown that socio-economic conditions of the mother like education, occupation, housing conditions, caste/ religion, family income have positive influence on the physical and mental health of the mother and inturn on her infant children. (Gopalan and Vijaya Raghavan, 1971: 2; Devdas, 1972: 23-24-; Acharya and Mitra, 1973:25; Vijaya Raghavan and Rao, 1973: 31; and UNICEF, 1974: 100-101).

Education of Mother

In many studies it is found that child mortality differentials are due to mother's education rather than the father's. It is based on the premise that the time and effort devoted to child care is greater by women than by men. Some studies have also revealed that child mortality in developing countries is associated more closely with maternal education than with any other socio-economic factors (Behe, 1979; Caldwell, 1979; Cochrene, 1980).

For our analysis, education of father and mother is classified into two categories only as literate and illiterate for the reason stated earlier. In the study area literacy is very low both among mothers and fathers (mothers 9 per cent and fathers 20 per cent), as mentioned earlier. From the table 3.6, it is observed that infant health and mother's literacy level are positively correlated; about 56.5 per cent of literate mothers have infants of normal health in contrast to 42.7 per cent of illiterates. Correspondingly 37.0 per cent of the infants of literate mothers have poor health, whereas it is 43.8 per cent among illiterates. It follows that a lower proportion of infants (6.5%) of literate mothers have very poor health compared to 13.5 per cent of those of illiterates. Thus, literacy of the mother has an influence on infant health. The chi-square test also reveals that the association between mother's education and

Table 3.6 Education of the Mother and Infant Health

Infant Health	*Literate*	*Illiterate*	*Total*
Normal	26 (56.5)	196 (42.7)	222
Poor	17 (37.0)	201 (43.8)	218
Very poor	3 (6.5)	62 (13.5)	65
Total	**46** **(100.0)**	**459** **(100.0)**	**505**

Note: Figures in the parentheses are in percentages.

infant health is significant at 5 per cent level of probability ($X^2 = 14.49$, $P < 0.05$ for 2 d.f).

Education of Father

Similar trend is observed with the educational level of fathers except that among the infants of poor health. But more than three times of infants of illiterate fathers have very poor health compare to those of literate fathers. In our study, mothers level of education does show better influence than that of fathers'. While about 56.5 per cent of infants are healthy when their mothers are literate, as against 50 per cent when their fathers are literate (Fig. 3.3). The gap between literate and illiterate mothers having healthy children is about

Table 3.7 Education of the Father and Infant Health

Infant Health	*Literate*	*Illiterate*	*Total*
Normal	51 (50.5)	171 (42.3)	222
Poor	45 (44.6)	173 (42.8)	218
Very poor	5 (4.9)	60 (14.9)	65
Total	**101** **(100.0)**	**404** **(100.0)**	**505**

Note: Figures in the parentheses are in percentages.

14 percentage points, as against 8 percentage points for fathers. This clearly indicates, the more mothers are literate, the more infants are healthy. The association between fathers education and infant health is statistically significant at 1 per cent level of probability ($X^2 = 11.4$, $P < 0.01$ for 2 d.f). These results are in conformity with other studies.

Occupation of Mother

The nature of women's occupation varies greatly both among and within societies. Reduction in maternal time devoted to child rearing may have an effect on infant health. The mother's activity status is believed to be an indicator of time spent in child rearing and domestic activities.

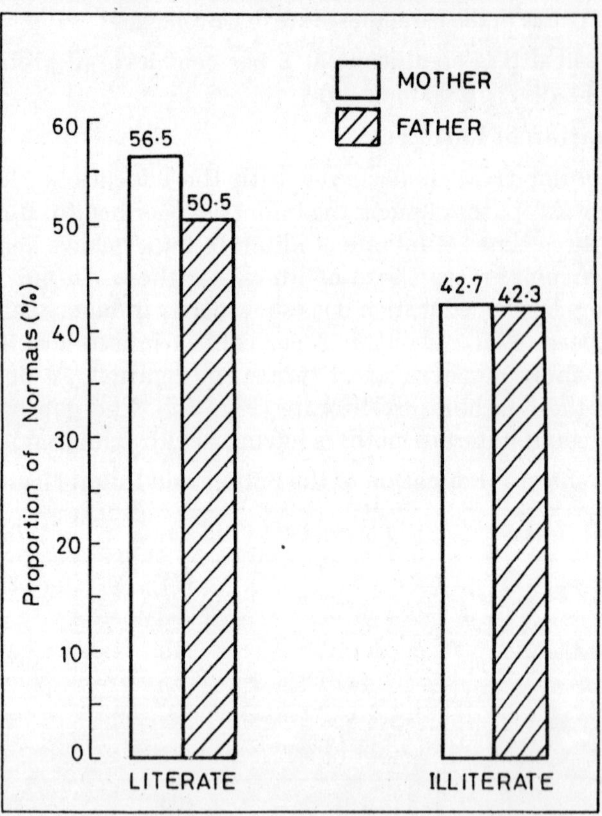

Fig. 3.3 Education of Mother and Father and Infant Health

Table 3.8 explains the status of infant health by mother's occupational level. The mother's occupational status is classified into two categories, namely worker and non-worker as mentioned earlier. In this study, about 75.4. per cent of the mothers are workers, 24.6 per cent of mothers are 'non-workers'. Thus, most of the women are working hard for their living. The health of the infant is almost similar, whether their mothers are 'workers (44.6%) or 'non-workers' (43.6%). The association between occupation of the mother and infant health is not statistically significant ($X^2 = 3.745$, p 70.05 for 2 d.f.).

Table 3.8 Occupation of the Mother and Infant Health

Infant Health	*Non-worker*	*Worker*	Total
Normal	54 (43.6)	168 (44.1)	222 (44.0)
Poor	48 (38.7)	170 (44.6)	218 (43.2)
Very poor	22 (17.7)	43 (11.3)	65 (12.9)
Total	**124** **(100.0)**	**381** **(100.0)**	**505** **(100.0)**

Note: Figures in the parentheses are in percentages.

Community (Caste/Religion)

Community is expected to have it's effect on infant health indirectly. Social and cultural habits and economic capacity regarding food intake, health care, etc., will vary from community to community. Generally it is expected that Forward Community people have better food intake, more health awareness and practice, than the other communities. Hence, in this chapter we would like to analyse influence of community on infant health. It is observed from Table 3.9, the highest proportion of infants in the Forward Community (52.4%) are of normal health, followed by infants of Scheduled Tribes (44.2%), Backward Community (42.3%) and of the Muslim Community (41.8%). The least proportion of normal infants is found among Scheduled Castes (38.5%). As mentioned in the earlier chapter, the Scheduled Caste community is economically and socially the lowest among all the communities. After Forward Community, it may appear surprising but infants of Scheduled Tribe have better health. The probable reason is among the Scheduled Tribes, it is observed that they have less taboo on foods during pregnancy and lactating time which are nutritious. They always do hard work, used to take raw food rich in nutrition, though not rich in cost. These habits will have its positive effect on infant health. This appears to be true in the study area. Highest proportion of infants of very poor health is found among Muslims (19.4%) followed by Scheduled Castes (16.7%) and Backward Community (13.2%). In general, among the five communities studied in the area, comparatively infants of the Forward Community have better health than the infants of other four communities. In this context , it is interesting to note that some of the Muslim women expressed that they are conceiving every year just because they are not being provided any type of birth control measures due to husband's opposition and non-cooperation.

Table 3.9 Community of the Mother and Infant Health

Infant Health	*F.C.*	*B.C.*	*S.C.*	*S.T.*	*Muslim*	*Total*
Normal	53 (52.5)	77 (42.3)	30 (38.5)	34 (44.2)	28 (41.8)	222
Poor	39 (38.6)	81 (44.5)	35 (48.7)	37 (48.1)	26 (38.8)	218
Very poor	9 (8.9)	24 (13.2)	13 (16.7)	6 (7.8)	13 (19.4)	65
Total	**101 (100.0)**	**182 (100.0)**	**78 (100.0)**	**77 (100.0)**	**67 (100.0)**	**505**

Note: 1. Figures in the parentheses are in percentages.
2. Forward Community (F.C), Backward Community (B.C), Scheduled Caste (S.C), Scheduled Tribe (S.T).

Annual Family Income

Economic aspects like income of the family has it's positive effect on infant's health if income is spent properly and purposfully. Income influences children's consumption of goods and services resulting in their health status. It is obviously reasonable to expect that a family with higher income should experience better child health due to availability of more health enhancing goods and services per capita than the children in lower income families. Therefore, income is one of the most powerful variable in determining the infant's health. But in the rural areas, estimating the annual income is very difficult. In spite of that, income is being assessed and classified into four groups according to the level of annual income per family. In the table 3.10, it is observed that with the increase in the level of income, the proportion of healthy infants increases from 38.5 per cent in income level of below Rs. 2000 to about 57 per cent in Rs. 6000 and above. Thus, as income increases the proportion of normal infants also increases (Fig. 3.4). The association between income and infant health is statistically significant at 5 per cent level of probability.

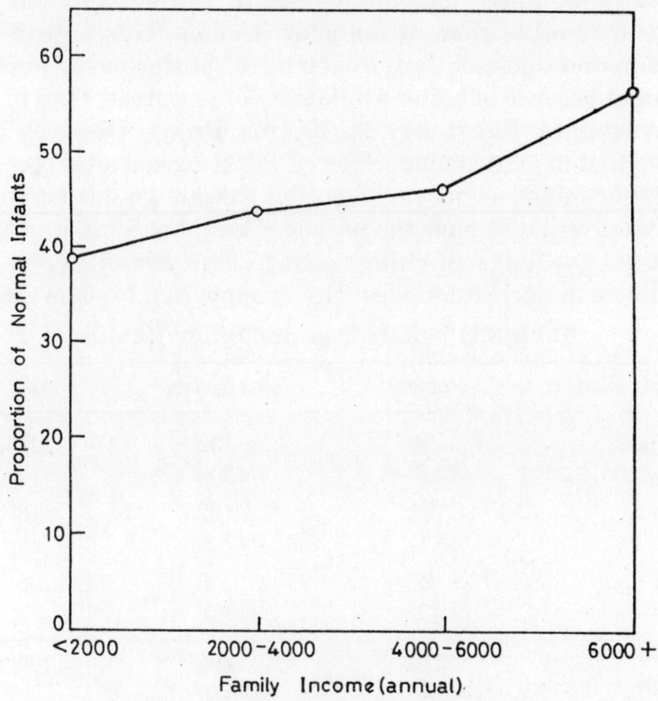

Fig. 3.4 Family Income and Infant Health (Proportion of Normals)

Table 3.10 Family Income and Infant Health

Infant Health	*Rs. 2000*	*Rs. 2000 4000*	*Rs. 4000 6000*	*Rs. 6000 +*	*Total*
Normal	37 (38.5)	136 (43.5)	26 (46.2)	23 (57.2)	222
Poor	44 (45.8)	144 (46.0)	19 (33.9)	11 (27.5)	218
Very poor	15 (15.6)	33 (10.5)	11 (19.6)	6 (15.0)	65
Total	**96 (100.0)**	**313 (100.0)**	**56 (100.0)**	**40 (100.0)**	**505**

(X^2 = 11.4, $P < 0.05$ for 6 d.f).
Note: Figures in the parentheses are in percentages.

Family Type and Infant Health

It is assumed that infant's health will be better in the nuclear families than in the joint families. This is with the assumption that childcare will be more satisfactory in nuclear families because of better availability of resources, than in the joint families. But it may not be true always. One may also argue that in joint families children will be looked after properly by other family members when the parents go out for work. Children will also have the benefit of grand parents who have better knowledge in child-rearing. This advantage is not available in nuclear families. This is supported to some extent

Table 3.11 Family Type and Infant Health

Infant Health	*Nuclear*	*Joint family*	*Total*
Normal	90 (42.3)	132 (45.2)	222
Poor	96 (45.1)	122 (41.8)	218
Very poor	27 (12.7)	38 (13.0)	65
Total	**213 (100.0)**	**292 (100.0)**	**505**

Note: Figures in the parentheses are in percentages

by the findings of our study. The proportion of healthy children is slightly more in joint family (45.2%). In nuclear family, 45.1 per cent of infants have poor health and 12.7 per cent of infants have very poor health. The corresponding figures in joint family are 41.8 per cent and 13.0 per cent (Table 3.11). However, the difference between family type and infant health is not statistically significant at 0.05 per cent level of probability ($X^2 = 0.56$, $P > 0.05$ for 2 d.f).

Infant's Attendant and Infant Health

Out of 505 infants surveyed, 51.1 per cent are male infants and 48.9 per cent are female infants. Out of these, 52.7 per cent of male infants and 38.5 per cent of female infants are looked after by their mother (Table 3.12); 24.4 per cent male and 30.4 per cent female infants are looked after by grand parents and the remaining 22.9 per cent male and 31.1 per cent female infants are looked after by others like relatives of mother or father. This shows that majority of male infants are looked after by their mother compared to female infants. Could this be preferential care for male infants compared to female infants by their mother? Though one is tempted to guess so, we can not say definitely, since we did not collect additional information in this regard. This can be explained partially due to the constitution of more male infants (25.6%) in the age group of 0-3 months compare to female infants in the same age group (20.2%).

Children attended by mothers personally are expected to be more healthy than those attended by others, mothers being more sincere and careful. However our results do not show any such differences, both in respect of male infants and female infants. Almost same proportion of male infants (about 46%) are healthy, whether they are attended by mothers or others (Table 3.12). Surprisingly, the proportion of healthy female infants is slightly higher among those attended by others (45.5%) than those attended by mothers (44.2%). Considering all infants (male and female together), there is no difference whether they are looked after by mothers or are looked after by others.

Table 3.12 Infant's Attendant and Infant Health

Infant's attendant	*Boys*				*Girls*				*Total*			
	Very poor	*Poor*	*Normal*	*Total*	*Very poor*	*Poor*	*Normal*	*Total*	*Very poor*	*Poor*	*Normal*	*Total*
Mother	20 (14.7)	53 (39.0)	63 (46.3)	136 (100.0)	12 (12.6)	41 (43.2)	42 (44.2)	95 (100.0)	32 (13.8)	94 (40.7)	105 (45.5)	231 (100.0)
Grand parents	8 (12.7)	29 (46.0)	26 (41.3)	63 (100.0)	11 (14.7)	34 (45.3)	30 (40.0)	75 (100.0)	19 (13.8)	63 (45.6)	56 (40.6)	138 (100.0)
Others	6 (10.2)	26 (44.0)	27 (45.8)	59 (100.0)	8 (10.4)	34 (44.2)	35 (45.5)	77 (100.0)	14 (10.3)	60 (44.1)	62 (45.6)	136 (100.0)
Total	**34**	**108**	**116**	**258**	**31**	**109**	**107**	**247**	**65**	**217**	**223**	**505**

Source: Figures in the brackets are in percentages.

DEMOGRAPHIC CHARACTERISTICS OF THE MOTHER

The demographic characteristics of the mother—age of the mother, age at marriage of the mother, infant deaths experienced by mother. have influence on infant health. In this section, these parameters have been studied.

Age of the Mother and Infant Health

Age of the mother has it's effects on the health of the infant. Generally, if the mother becomes pregnant or delivers a baby at a proper age, that is say, after 18 years, the health of the infant would be better than the baby's whose mother's age is below 18 years. The maternal age (too early, or too late, after 35 years of age) is strongly correlated with congenital malformations among children. This relationship has been documented in the literature in many countries, especially for Down's Syndrome (Mongolism) WHO, (1976). Yerushalmy (1945) found that the risk of still births was high for young mothers (under 20 years), declined for mothers aged 20 to 29, and rose thereafter with maternal age. Data on late foetal deaths reported to the World Health Organisation by eight countries confirm the 'U' shaped or 'J' shaped relationship with maternal age (WHO, 1971).

Table 3.13 Age of the Respondent and Infant Health

Infant Health	*Age of the Respondent*			
	15-19	*20-29*	*30+*	*Total*
Normal	38 (50.7)	146 (44.4)	38 (37.6)	222
Poor	31 (41.3)	140 (42.6)	47 (46.5)	218
Very	6 (8.0)	43 (13.0)	16 (15.8)	65
Total	**75** **(100.0)**	**329** **(100.0)**	**101** **(100.0)**	**505**

Source: Figures in the breakfasts are in perembages.
Note: $X^2 = 5.94$, $P < 0.05$ for 2 d.f.

In this section, the infant's health is analysed in relation to their mother's age at the time of survey. The data show that the present age of mother has effect on infant health (Table 3.13). It is observed that young mothers (15-19 years) have healthier children than that of old mothers (30 years and above). Among young mothers (15-19 years) 50.7 per cent of their infants have normal health.

The corresponding figures for middle aged (20-29 years) and for old mothers (30 years and above) are about 44 and 38 per cent respectively. Thus, there is a decline of level of infant's health as mother's age advances. This may be due to deteriorating nutritional status of mothers, repeated pregnancies and also due to poor economic conditions. The 20-29 years of age is normally considered as ideal age of motherhood with reference to infant health. In our study, this is examined for 20-24 and 25-29 years of age groups separately, since no difference was found between them, the results for 20-29 age group are presented in the table 3.13.

Age at Marriage of the Mother and Infant Health

Among the infants whose mother's age at marriage is less than 18 years, 43.9 per cent of them are healthy, the same proportion of them have poor health, and 12.2 per cent of them have very poor health (Table 3.14). Among the infants whose mother's age at marriage is 18 years and above 44.2 per cent of infants are healthy, 40.7 per cent have poor health, and 15.0 per cent have very poor health. In this study, thus, it is found that there is no relationship between mother's age at marriage and health of the infant (77.6 per cent of the respondent's have married before 18 years of age). In other words, besides age at marriage on motherhood, there are other more important determinants of infants health at least in study area. This may be due to the fact that age at marriage is more relevant to the health of the first child rather than the subsequent children, since it was thought age at first pregnancy could have been more relevant, same was also examined, but there was no difference in the pattern.

Table 3.14 Age at Marriage of the Respondent and Infant Health

Infant Health	*Age at marriage (Years)*		
	18	*18+*	*Total*
Normal	172 (43.9)	50 (44.2)	222
Poor	172 (43.9)	46 (40.7)	218
Very poor	48 (12.2)	8 (15.0)	65
Total	**392** **(100.0)**	**113** **(100.0)**	**505**

$X^2 = 3.23$ P = >0.05 for 2 d.f.

Note: Figures in the parentheses are in percentages.

Number of Infant Deaths Experienced by the Mother and Infant Health

Usually, infant health will be better whose mother has not experienced any infant death which indicates better health for mother. In the present study, 31.3 per cent of mothers have experienced at least one infant death (Table 3.15). The health

Table 3.15 Infant Deaths Experienced by the Mother and Infant Health

Infant Health	*Infant deaths not experienced*	*Infant deaths experienced*	*Total*
Normal	157 (45.2)	65 (41.1)	222
Poor	153 (44.1)	65 (41.1)	218
Very poor	37 (10.7)	28 (17.7)	65
Total	**347** **(100.0)** **(68.7)**	**158** **(100.0)** **(31.3)**	**505** **(100.0)** **(100.0)**

$x^2 = 6.10$, p^2 0.05 for 2 d.f.

Note: Figures in the parentheses are in percentages

status of infants whose mothers have not experienced infant deaths is slightly better (45.2%) compared to the infants whose mothers experienced infant deaths (41.1%). Similarly, the proportion of infants who are of very poor health, is considerably higher (17.7%) among mothers who experienced infant deaths than those who did not (10.7%). The association between infant deaths experienced by the mother and infant health is statistically significant.

FOOD AND NUTRITION OF THE MOTHER AND CHILD

In this section, infant health is discussed in relation to food and nutrition of the mother. Health of the infant depends upon nutrition of the mother. In this study, food and nutrition of mother is measured in terms of additional foods taken or avoided during pregnancy and lactation, and adequacy of breast milk. Feeding pattern of infants in the first three days and supplementary food given to infants are also discussed.

Additional Foods Taken During Pregnancy

A woman needs engough food to keep herself healthy and if she becomes pregnant she needs additional food to enable the foetus to grow normally in the womb, because, her nutrition has a direct relationship to birth weight. It follows, therefore, that for infants to be healthy, the mother should also be healthy. One of the major factors that promotes health both of the mother and the baby in the womb is nourishing food. Hence, the necessity of the additional energy allowance, during pregnancy and lactation in the second and third trimester of 300 kcal/day, and in the first six months of lactation 550 kcal/ day and the next six months 400 kcal/day (ICMR, 1981). But only 18.2 per cent of women have reported that they have taken 'additional' foods during pregnancy in this study area. Even that additional food was not much, possibly because of their poverty.

In the study area, about 48.0 per cent of infants are normal among women who have taken additional foods during pregnancy. Among women who have not taken additional foods, 44.1 per cent are normal. However, it is not statistically significant ($X^2 = 3.71$, $P > 0.05$ for 2 d.f.) Due to poor economic conditions they are not taking sufficient quantity of food during normal time, that is when they are not pregnant.

Table 3.16 Number of Respondents by Additional Food taken during Pregnancy and Infant Health

Infant health	*Special foods taken during pregnancy*		
	Yes	*No*	*Total*
Normal	44 (47.8)	182 (44.1)	222
Poor	32 (34.8)	182 (44.1)	218
Very poor	16 (17.4)	49 (11.8)	65
Total	**92** **(100.0) (18.2)**	**413** **(100.0) (81.8)**	**505** **(100.0) (100.0)**

Note: Figures in the parentheses are in percentages.

Additional Foods Taken During Lactation

As already mentioned earlier, breast-feeding imposes a greater strain than pregnancy on the mother and therefore, her nutritional needs are higher than those during pregnancy. Lactating woman must take more food than pregnant and

Table 3.17 Number of Respondents by Additional Foods taken during Lactation and Infant Health

Infant Health	*Special foods taken during lactation*		
	Yes	*No*	*Total*
Normal	20 (47.6)	206 (44.5)	222
Poor	18 (42.9)	196 (42.3)	218
Very poor	4 (9.5)	61 (13.2)	65
Total	**42** **(100.0) (8.3)**	**463** **(100.0) (91.7)**	**505** **(100.0) (100.0)**

Note: Figures in the parentheses are in percentages.

ordinary woman. She needs more food for better lactation and also to maintain good health. In this study, only 8.3 per cent have taken additional foods during lactation such as meat and fish. About 47.6 per cent of the infants are normal among women who consumed additional foods during the period of lactation and 44.5 per cent of infants are normal among women who have not taken additional foods, showing little difference between these two. The difference is not statistically significant. ($X^2 = 0.62$, $P>0.05$ for 2 d.f.).

Foods Avoided During Pregnancy

There are no restrictions on any particular foods to be taken by the pregnant women (NIN, 1979). But, too much of condiments and foods which habitually disagree with the system should be avoided, and also foods which are of strong odours or those which leave a taste long after eaten should be avoided as they may bring on an attack of nausea (Venkatachalam, and Rebello, 1978). However, good foods avoided during pregnancy has adverse influence on health of the child.

In the study area, because of superstition, certain foods are avoided during pregnancy such as papaya, brinjal, mango, green chillies, jack fruit, pumpkin, etc. They believe that these are hot foods and may cause abortion. About 47.0 per cent of the respondents have avoided the above said foods. Among women who avoided certain foods during pregnancy, 41.6 per cent of their infants are normal and among the women who did not avoid any food during their pregnancy period 46.1 per cent are normal (Table 3.18). About 18.9 per cent infants are very poor in health among those women who avoided some foods during pregnancy compared to 7.5 per cent of infants of those women who have not avoided foods during pregnancy. This shows significant influence on infant health of avoiding nutritious food during pregnancy. It is statistically significant ($X^2 = 14.8$, $P < 0.01$ for 2 d.f.).

Foods Avoided During Lactation

Similarly certain foods also are avoided during lactation period. The foods that are avoided during lactation are:

Table 3.18 Number of Respondents Avoided Some Foods During Pregnancy and Infant Health

Infant Health	Food avoided during pregnancy		
	Yes	*No*	*Total*
Normal	99 (41.6)	123 (46.1)	222
Poor	94 (37.5)	124 (46.4)	218
Very Poor	45 (18.9)	20 (7.5)	65
Total	**238** **(100.0)** **(47. 1)**	**267** **(100.0)** **(52.9)**	**505** **(100.0)** **(100.0)**

Note: Figures in the parentheses are in percentages.

pappaya, brinjal, jaggery, mango, black grape, green chillies, beans, banana, plantains, cucumber, butter milk, potato, sweet potato, jack fruit, pumpkin, coconut, gava, mushrooms, red gram dal, cheese, chicken, sheep meat, eggs, etc. The reasons for avoiding these foods are due to the belief that mother and also child will suffer from cold, cough and fever, some women

Table 3.19 Number of Respondents Avoided Certain Food During Lactation and Infant Health

Infant Health	Food avoided during Lactation		
	Yes	*No*	*Total*
Normal	67 (39.9)	55 (46.0)	222
Poor	77 (45.8)	141 (41.8)	218
Very Poor	24 (14.3)	41 (12.2)	65
Total	**168** **(100.0)** **(33.3)**	**337** **(100.0)** **(66.7)**	**505** **(100.0)** **(100.0)**

Note: Figures in the parentheses are in percentages.

also said that children will not survive, if these foods are eaten. Interestingly, among the Scheduled Tribes most of them said that they have not avoided any foods and very few said that they have avoided chicken and sheep meat. In other communities, at the time of lactation most of the women used to take only rice and rasam (water boiled with tamarind and spices) not at all a nutritious food to meet the demand of both mother and child.

From the table 3.19 it is observed that in the study area about 33.3 per cent of women have avoided certain foods during lactation. Among women who avoided food during lactation period, 39.9 per cent of infants are normal compared to 46.0 per cent of infants whose mothers have not avoided foods during lactation. About 14.3 per cent of infants have very poor health among mothers who have avoided food during lactation compared to 12.2 per cent of infants whose mothers have not avoided food during lactation. The proportion of respondents avoided certain foods during pregnency period (47.1%) is more than during lactation period (33.1%).

Feeding Pattern of Infant in the First Three Days and Infant Health

Infant feeding begins immediately after birth and it varies from mother to mother because of different social and educational background. Breast milk should be given to the baby as the first feed after the delivary of the baby. The first secretion contains colostrum and it works as an antibiotic for the baby. But in the survey, it is observed that various types of feeds are in practice, namely sugar water, honey, cow's milk, other lactating mother's milk, and castor oil. The highest proportion of babies are given castor oil as the first feed (47.9%), followed by sugar water (43.0%), other lactating mother's milk (5.1%), cow's milk (2.0%), and honey (0.4%) (Table 3.20). Only 1.6 per cent of the babies are given the breast milk. Among the communities, feeding castor oil is highest among Scheduled Tribes (97.4%) followed by Scheduled Castes (62.8%), and lowest proportion is found to be among Muslims (4.5%). Feeding sugar

Table 3.20 Feeding Pattern of Infants in the First Three Days, by Caste/Religion

Caste / Religion	*Castor oil*	*Sugar water*	*Other lactating mothers milk*	*Animal milk*	*Breast milk*	*Honey*	*Total*
Forward Community	24 (23.8)	69 (68.3)	4 (4.0)	—	3 (.3.0)	1 (1.0)	101 (100.0)
Backward Community	87 (47.2)	73 (40.1)	13 (7.1)	4 (2.2)	4 (2.2)	1 (0.5)	132 (100.0)
Scheduled Castes	49 (62.8)	21 (26.9)	6 (7.7)	1 (1.3)	1 (1.3)	—	78 (100.0)
Scheduled Tribes	75 (97.4)	2 (2.6)	—	—	—	—	77 (100.0)
Muslims	7 (10.4)	52 (77.6)	3 (4.5)	5 (7.5)	—	—	67 (100.0)
Total	**8** **(1.6)**	**2** **(0.1)**	**217** **(43.0)**	**10** **(2.0)**	**26** **(5.1)**	**242** **(47.9)**	**505** **(100.0)**

Note: Figures in the parentheses are in percentages,

water is highest among Muslims (77.6%) and Forward Castes (68.3%). Other lactating mother's milk is highest among Scheduled Castes (7.7%) and Backward Castes (7.1%) and it is usually due to mother's illness or breast problem. In the present analysis this aspect is not examined as only a very few babies are given breast milk as the first feed (out of 505 babies, only eight were given breast milk). This may be due to lack of knowledge and awareness of the benefits of the first secretion of the breast milk among respondents.

Adequacy of Breast Milk and Infant Health

The respondents were enquired about their perception of adequacy of breast milk for their infants. In the study, it is observed that only 14.7 per cent of the total respondents answered that they do have more (surplus) breast milk. (Table 3.21). About 46.7 per cent of the respondents said that they have sufficient milk and the remaining 38.6 per cent said that they have less (inadequate) milk.

Table 3.21 Adequacy of Breast Milk and Infant Health

Infant Health	*Breast milk*			*Total*
	Inad.	*Suff.*	*Surp.*	
Normal	71 (36.4)	114 (48.3)	37 (50.0)	222
Poor	91 (46.7)	93 (39.4)	34 (45.9)	218
Very Poor	33 (16.9)	29 (12.3)	3 (4.1)	65
Total	**195** **(100.0)** **(38.6)**	**236** **(100.0)** **(46.7)**	**74** **(100.0)** **(14.7)**	**505**

Note: Figures in the parentheses are in percentages
1. Inad: Inadequate, 2. Suff: Sufficient, 3. Surp: Surplus

Adequacy of breast milk and infant health by age of the infant is discussed in table 3.22 (*See on next page*). In this table, mothers of sufficient and surplus milk is added and kept as mothers of adequate milk.

From the table 3.22, one can observe that in all age groups of infants, the proportion of normal infants are more with

Table 3.22 Adequacy of Breast-Milk and Infant Health by Age of the Infant

Infant Health	*Infant Age*											
	0-2			*3-5*			*6-8*			*9-11*		
	Inad.	*Adeq.*	*Total*	*Inad*	*Adeq.*	*Total*	*Inad.*	*Adq.*	*Total*	*Ind*	*Adeq.*	*Total*
Normal	13 (54.2)	24 (51.1)	37	18 (36.0)	41 (62.1)	59	27 (41.5)	51 (58.6)	78	13 (23.2)	35 (31.8)	48
Poor	8 (33.3)	18 (38.3)	26	25 (50.0)	21 (31.8)	46	26 (40.0)	31 (35.6)	57	32 (57.1)	57 (51.8)	89
Very Poor	3 (12.5)	5 (10.6)	8	7 (14.0)	4 (6.1)	11	12 (18.5)	5 (5.8)	17	11 (19.6)	18 (16.4)	29
Total	**24 (100.0) (33.8)**	**47 (100.0) (66.2)**	**71**	**50 (100.0) (43.1)**	**66 (100.0) (56.9)**	**116**	**65 (100.0) (42.8)**	**87 (100.0) (57.2)**	**152**	**56 (100.0) (33.7)**	**110 (100.0) (66.3)**	**166**
	100			**100**			**100**			**100**		

Note: Figures in the parentheses are in percentage
1. Inad: Inadequate, 2. Suff: Sufficient, 3. Surp: Surplus

mothers of adequate milk compare to mothers of inadequate milk except in the first age group (0-2 months). The proportion of normal infants with adequate mother's milk in the age group 3-5 months is 62.1 per cent. This proportion declined to 58.0 per cent in the age group of 6-8 months and further declined more to 31.8 per cent in the age group of 9-11 months. It has declined though they have adequate milk. It may be due to not providing supplementary foods after completion of five months of age either due to ignorence or inability. Similarly, in all age groups of infants, the proportion of poor and very poor health of infants are more with mothers of inadequate milk.

Supplementary Foods given and Infant Health

Supplementary feeding with adequate amount of nutrients should be introduced 4 to 5 months age without stopping breast-feeding. In the study area, it is observed that the supplementary foods are not properly given to infants. In total, about 44.2 per cent of the infants are given supplementary foods (*Table 3.23*). The supplementary foods that are given to children are: sariganji, (boiled rice chunned/grounded in water), rice, sangati (food prepared with ragi and rice), Amul milk powder and Farex. Only a few infants in the age group of 3-5 months are given supplementary foods (27.6%). From six months and after, giving supplementary foods has gradually increased. If for any reason mothers have no breast milk, then only the infants are fed with cow/buffalow milk. After sixth month most of the infants are given supplementary food in a ceremony on auspicious day. The proportion of infants receiving supplementary foods in the age group of 6-8 months is 47.8 per cent, in the age group of 9-11 months 70.5 per cent. Fifty seven per cent of the infants are given supplementary foods at age sixth month and over. Highest proportion are given rice or sangati (25.2%), followed by sariganji (5.3%), Amul milk powder or Farex (3.8%). In the study, it is found that there is no significant relationship between supplementary foods given and infant health ($X^2 = 9.4$, $P > 0.05$ for 4 d.f). The respondents have little knowledge about the quantity and quality of the supplementary foods to be given to infants. In the study areas, when the elders are eating in the family they just provide the same food to the infants, and they do not bother much whether the infant was fed properly or not.

Table 3.23 Age of the Infant, Supplementary Food Given or Not Given and Infant Health

Age of the Infant	*Supplementary Food*								
	Not given				*Given*				
	Very poor	*Poor*	*Normal*	*Total*	*Very poor*	*Poor*	*Normal*	*Total*	*G. Total*
0-2	6 (9.7)	23 (37.1)	33 (53.2)	62 (100.0) (87.3)	2 (22.2)	3 (33.3)	4 (44.5)	9 (100.0) (12.7)	71 (100.0) (100.0)
3-5	5 (6.0)	33 (39.3)	46 (54.7)	84 (100.0) (72.4)	5 (15.6)	13 (40.6)	14 (46.8)	32 (100.0) (27.6)	116 (100.0) (100.0)
6-8	9 (10.3)	35 (40.3)	43 (49.4)	87 (100.0) (57.2)	9 (13.8)	21 (32.3)	35 (53.9)	65 (100.0) (47.8)	152 (100.0) (100.0)
9-11	10 (20.4)	27 (55.1)	12 (24.5)	49 (100.0) (29.5)	19 (16.3)	63 (53.8)	35 (29.1)	117 (100.0) (70.5)	166 (100.0) (100.0)
Total	**30** **(10.6)**	**118** **(41.9)**	**134** **(47.5)** **(55.8)**	**282** **(100.0)**	**35** **(15.7)**	**100** **(44.8)**	**88** **(34.5)** **(44.2)**	**223** **(100.0)** **(100.0)**	**505** **(100.0)**

Note: Figures in the parentheses are in percentages.

Weight of Women

Weight of a woman has influence on infant health. In the study area, the average weight of a woman is 40.97 kilograms, with a standard deviation of 5.47 kilograms. It is very surprising to know that among the respondents, there are two women whose weight is just 29 kilograms each. About 41.0 per cent of women have weight below 40 kilograms.

From table 3.24, one can observe that among mothers whose weight is 50 kilograms and above have 57.6 per cent of infants are of normal health, compare to those mothers whose weight is 40-49 kilograms and also among mothers whose weight is less than 40 kilograms have 46.0 per cent and 39.1 per cent of infants are of normal health respectively. However, there is no association between weight of a woman and infant health ($X^2 = 4.56$, $P > 0.05$, for 2 d.f). Due to poverty many women are unable to eat the required amount of food, hence the low weight.

Table 3.24 Weight of the Respondent and Infant Health

Weight (K.gms)	*Infant health*					
	Very poor	*Poor*	*Normal*	*Total*	*Percentage*	*Cumulative percentage*
<40	31 (15.0)	95 (45.9)	81 (39.1)	207 (100.0)	41.0	41.0
40-49	32 (12.1)	111 (41.9)	122 (46.0)	265 (100.0)	52.5	93.5
≥50	2 (6.1)	12 (36.3)	19 (57.6)	33 (100.0)	6.5	100.0
Total	**65**	**218**	**222**	**505**	**100.0**	

Note: Figures in the parentheses are in percentages

Height of Women

In the study area, height of a woman is also measured. A woman whose height is better will have easy delivery and less complications due to delivery. In the study area, the average height of a woman is 151.9 centimeters.

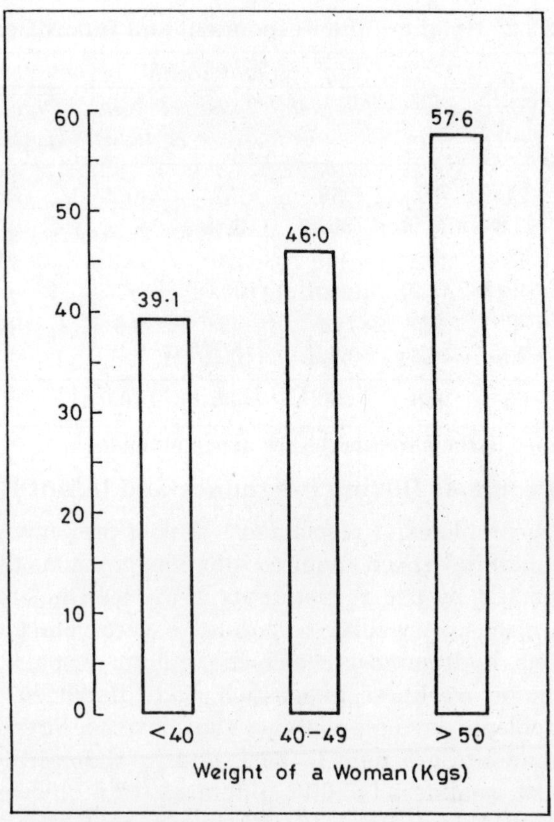

Fig. 3.5 Weight of a Woman and Infant Health (proportion of normals)

From the table 3.25, one can observe that tall women (whose height is 160-174 cms) have higher proportion of normal infants (51.2%) compare to short women (whose height is 135 to 149 cms) have lower proportion of normal infants (36.2%). However, X^2 -test reveals that there is no association between height of a woman and infant health. ($X^2 = 4.43$, $P > 0.01$ for 2 d.f.).

HEALTH OF MOTHER

In this section, infant health is discussed in relation to health of the mother. Health of the infant depends upon health of the mother. In this study, health of the mother is measured in terms of complications during pregnancy, complications during post-natal period, and personal hygiene.

Table 3.25 Height of the Respondent and Infant Health

Weight (c.ms)	*Infant health*					
	Very poor	*Poor*	*Normal*	*Total*	*Percen-tage*	*Cumulative percentage*
135-149	21 (13.8)	76 (50.0)	55 (36.2)	152 (100.0)	30.2	30.2
150-159	43 (12.1)	122 (41.9)	145 (46.0)	310 (100.0)	60.3	91.5
160-174	1 (2.3)	20 (46.5)	22 (51.2)	43 (100.0)	9.5	100.0
Total	**65**	**218**	**222**	**505**	**100.0**	

Note: Figures in the parentheses are in percentages

Health Problems During Pregnancy and Infant Health

Health problems of respondents during pregnancy of the present infant have been enquired into. The problems that have been reported by the respondents are: bleeding, toxemia, systemic diseases, swelling of hands," severe vomiting, B.P., convulsions, hydromniosis, headache, giddiness, pain in back and abdomine, weakness, indigestion, acute diarrhoea, etc. The health problems during pregnancy that have been reported by the respondents are pain in back and in abdomin (45.5%), followed by weakness (45.0%), giddiness (42.6%), swelling of hands (38.2%), indigestion (34.5%), severe vomiting (30.5%), bleeding (18.0%), and hydromniosis (12.9%) accute diarrhoea (8.9%), and systomic diseases (5.5%), etc. (Table 3.26).

Complications during pregnancy and infant health is presented in table 3.27 (*See on page 100*). The general hypothesis is that 'more the complications during pregnancy lower is the health of the infant'. In the study area, about 30.5 per cent of the respondents did not have complications (mentioned earlier) during their last pregnancy (Table 3.27). About 26.9 per cent of the respondents had 1 to 3 complications, and the remaining 42.6 per cent had more than five complications. In this study, it is found that there is no association between complications during pregnancy and infant health ($X^2 = 0.83$, $P > 0.05$ for 1 d.f.). Moreover, it is not easy to relate health problem during pregnancy and infant health, because even after birth, infants health can be improved by other health care measures. There may be recall lapse on the part of respondents also.

Table 3.26 Specific Health Problems During Pregnancy and Infant Health

Complication During Pregnancy	*Infant Health*							
	Normal 222		*Poor 218*		*Very poor 65*		*Total 505*	
	Yes	*No*	*Yes*	*No*	*Yes*	*No*	*Yes*	*No*
1. Bleeding	39 (43.8)	183 (44.0)	37 (40.7)	181 (43.7)	13 (14.3)	52 (12.6)	89 (17.6)	416 (82.4)
2. Toxemia	7 (53.8)	215 (43.7)	6 (46.2)	212 (43.1)	—	65 (13.2)	13 (2.6)	492 (97.4)
3. Systomic diseases	12 (46.4)	210 (43.9)	10 (35.7)	208 (43.6)	5 (17.9)	60 (12.6)	27 (5.3)	478 (94.7)
4. Swelling of hands	91 (48.7)	136 (42.7)	78 (40.4)	140 (44.9)	23 (11.9)	42 (13.5)	187 (37.0)	318 (63.0)
5. Severe vomiting	67 (43.5)	155 (44.2)	69 (44.8)	149 (42.5)	18 (11.7)	47 (13.4)	154 (30.5)	351 (69.5)
6. High or Low B.P	3 (42.9)	219 (44.0)	3 (42.9)	215 (43.2)	1 (14.3)	64 (12.9)	7 (1.4)	498 (98.6)
7. Convul-sions	10 (58.8)	215 (43.4)	5 (29.4)	213 (43.6)	2 (11.8)	63 (12.9)	17 (3.4)	488 (96.6)
8. Hydrom-niosis	24 (36.9)	198 (45.0)	28 (43.1)	190 (43.2)	13 (20.0)	52 (11.8)	65 (12.9)	440 (87.1)
9. Headache	92 (43.2)	130 (43.3)	91 (43.5)	127 (42.9)	22 (10.5)	43 (14.5)	205 (40.6)	300 (59.4)
10. Giddiness	94 (44.5)	128 (40.8)	91 (42.3)	127 (43.8)	26 (11.7)	39 (14.5)	205 (40.6)	300 (59.4)
11. Pain in back and abdomen	105 (45.7)	117 (42.5)	98 (42.6)	120 (43.6)	27 (43.8)	28 (11.7)	230 (13.8)	275 (54.5)
12. Weakness	104 (45.8)	118 (42.4)	93 (41.0)	125 (45.0)	30 (13.2)	35 (12.6)	227 (45.0)	278 (55.0)
13. Indigestion	76 (43.7)	146 (44.1)	76 (43.7)	142 (42.9)	22 (12.6)	43 (13.0)	174 (34.5)	331 (65.5)
14. Acute Dirrhoea	17 (37.8)	205 (44.6)	18 (40.0)	200 (43.5)	10 (22.2)	55 (11.9)	45 (8.9)	460 (91.1)
15. Others	13 (56.5)	209 (43.4)	8 (34.8)	210 (43.6)	2 (8.7)	63 (13.1)	23 (4.6)	482 (95.4)

Note: Figures in the parentheses are in percentages

Table 3.27 Complications During Pregnancy and Infant Health

Infant Health	*No complications*	*One or more complications*	*Total*
Normal	43 (28.4)	159 (71.6)	222 (100.0)
Not normal	91 (32.2)	192 (67.8)	283 (100.0)
Total	**154 (30.5)**	**351 (69.5)**	**505 (100.0)**

$X^2 = 0.83$, $p > 0.05$ for 1 d.f.
Note: Figures in the parentheses are in percentages

Complications in the Post-natal Period

The complications that have been reported in the study by the respondents are: body pains, backache, weakness, fever, breast pain, diarrhoea, stomach discomfort, stomach pain, chest pain, indigestion, etc. For major part of their post-natal period, about 29.9 per cent of women suffered from one or two of these complications. Women who have not suffered with any complication have more normal infants (45.7%) compared to the women who have suffered from one or two post-natal complications (39.7%), as shown in table 3.28. It is also statistically significant ($X^2 = 7.93$, $P < 0.05$ for 2 d.f.).

Table 3.28 Number of Respondents with Complications in Post-natal Period and Infant Health

Infant Health	*Post-natal complications*		
	No	*Yes*	*Total*
Normal	162 (45.7)	60 (39.7)	222
Poor	156 (44.1)	62 (41.1)	218
Very poor	36 (10.2)	29 (19.2)	65
Total	**354 (100.0) (70.1)**	**151 (100.0) (29.9)**	**505 (100.0) (100.0)**

Note: Figures in the parentheses are in percentages.

Personal Hygiene of the Mother and Infant Health

Personal hygiene for the present analysis is considered by mother taking bath. From the table 3.29, one can observe that in the study area, about 4.7 per cent of the respondents do not take bath even once in a weak, and 64.4 per cent of the respondents take bath only once in a week. Taking bath twice, thrice and four to seven times in a week are 21.0 per cent, 4.2 per cent, 5.7 per cent respectively (Table 3.29). Though it is found that there is no consistent relationship between infant health and bathing of the respondents, higher proportion of infants (about 55 per cent) are healthy among women taking bath 4-7 times a week, as against 43 per cent of infants of women not taking bath even once in a week.

Table 3.29 Frequency of Bath Per Week and Infant Health

Infant	*Bath per week*					
Health	*Not even once*	*Once*	*Twice*	*Thrice*	*4-7 times*	*Total*
Normal	11 (42.8)	142 (43.7)	43 (40.6)	10 (47.6)	16 (55.2)	222
Poor	12 (50.0)	145 (44.6)	44 (41.5)	8 (38.1)	9 (31.0)	218
Very poor	1 (4.2)	38 (11.7)	19 (17.9)	3 (14.3)	4 (13.8)	65
Total	**24** **(100.0)** **(4.7)**	**325** **(100.0)** **(64.4)**	**106** **(100.0)** **(21.0)**	**21** **(100.0)** **(4.2)**	**29** **(100.0)** **(5.7)**	**505** **(100.0)** **(100.0)**

$X^2 = 1.96$, P =>0.05, for 4 d.f.

Note: Figures in parentheses are in percentages

HEALTH SERVICES AND INFANT HEALTH

Health services have greater influence on infant health. The variables that are considered under the health services are medical check-up during pregnancy, place of delivery conducted, immunisation to infant, and family planning.

Place of Last Delivery Conducted and Infant Health

Place of delivery conducted is an important variable that has influence on infant health. In the study area, most of the deliveries are conducted at home (90.3%), and only about 10 per cent of the deliveries are conducted at private hospital, Primary Health Centre (PHC), and district hospital. Among the infants delivered at home, about 43.9 per cent of infants are normal in health, compared to 44.9 per cent of infants who were delivered in hospital (Table 3.30). There is no difference in the health of the infants whether delivery conducted at home or hospital. But many diseases can be avoided and health of the infant can be improved, if the delivery is conducted in the hospital.

Table 3.30 Place of Delivery and Infant Health

Infant Health	*Place of delivery*		
	Hospital	*Home*	*Total*
Normal	22 (44.9)	200 (43.9)	222
Poor	22 (44.9)	196 (43.0)	218
Very poor	5 (10.2)	60 (13.1)	65
Total	**49** **(100.0)** **(9.7)**	**456** **(100.0)** **(90.3)**	**505** **(100.0)**

$X^2 = 0.37$, $P > 0.01$ for 2 d.f.

Note: Figures in the parentheses are in percentages

Medical Check-up During Pregnancy and Infant Health

Medical check-up during pregnancy is essential to ensure safe delivery and proper growth and development of the child. In this study, about 44.9 per cent of the respondents had medical check-up during their pregnancy at least once (Table 3.31). About 44.1 per cent of the infants, whose mothers had medical check-up during pregnancy at least once have normal health, as against 43.9 per cent of the infants whose mother's did not have medical check-up during pregnancy revealing no association between the two. But 45.4 per cent of the infants whose mothers have medical check-up three and more times are normal in contrast to about 39 per cent of infants whose

Table 3.31 Medical Check-up During Pregnancy and Infant Health

Infant Health	*Medical Check-up*					
	No Check up	*One time*	*Two time*	*Three & more Times*	*Total*	*Grand Total*
Normal	122 (43.9)	22 (38.6)	14 (48.3)	64 (45.4)	100 (44.1)	222 (44.0)
Poor	127 (45.7)	23 (40.4)	8 (27.6)	60 (42.6)	91 (40.1)	218 (43.2)
Very poor	29 (10.4)	12 (21.1)	7 (24.1)	17 (12.1)	36 (15.8)	65 (12.9)
Total	**278 (100.0) (55.1)**	**57 (100.0) (11.3)**	**29 (100.0) (5.7)**	**141 (100.0) (27.9)**	**227 (100.0) (44.9)**	**505 (100.0) (100.0)**

Note: Figures in the parentheses are in percentages

mothers had medical check-up only once. Thus, medical check-up during pregnancy has influence on infant health only when they have medical check-up regularly. But it is surprising to note that more infants of mothers without any medical check-up were healthy, than those who had medical check-up only once. The only probable reason for the paradox is, those who had medical check-up once might not have followed the directions of doctors either due to poverty or lack of seriousness, and defects remained without treatment and their infants were affected. In other words, it is not just medical check-up but it is the utilisation of services which will secure health for both mother and child.

Immunisation and Infant Health

Immunisation is very essential to prevent certain diseases of children. BCG, DPT, and Polio drops will be given to infants to prevent tuberculosis, diphtheria, purtosis, tetanus and polio respectively. Considerable proportion of children are suffering due to these diseases. In the study area, 37.0 per cent of infants are immunised against BCG, 36 per cent against DPT, and only 27 per cent against polio. Moreover, they are not given in the required doses. Among the infants who had been given BCG,

Table 3.32 Immunisation (BCG) and Infant Health

Infant Health	*BCG*		
	Not given	*Given*	*Total*
Normal	135 (42.5)	87 (46.5)	222
Poor	140 (44.0)	78 (41.7)	218
Very poor	43 (13.5)	22 (11.8)	65
Total	**318** **(100.0)** **(63.0)**	**187** **(100.0)** **(37.0)**	**505** **(100.0)**

$X^2 = 0.87$, $P > 0.05$ for 2 d.f.
Note: Figures in the parentheses are in percentages

Table 3.33 Immunisation (DPT) and Infant Health

Infant Health	*DPT*		
	Not given	*Given*	*Total*
Normal	138 (42.9)	84 (45.9)	222
Poor	142 (44.1)	76 (41.5)	218
Very poor	42 (13.0)	23 (12.6)	65
Total	**322** **(100.0)** **(63.4)**	**183** **(100.0** **(36.6)**	**505** **(100.0)**

$X^2 = 0.35$, $P > 0.05$ for 2 d.f.
Note: Figures in the parentheses are in percentages

about 46.2 per cent are normal as against 42 per cent infants who did not recieve BCG. Similarly, about 45.9 per cent of infants are normal who have received D.P.T., compare to 42.9 per cent who have not received D.P.T. Among the polio vaccine receivers, 45.6 per cent of infants are normal compared to 43.4 per cent of infants who have not received the polio vaccine. In general, in the present study, there is no significant difference in proportion of normal infants between those immunised and not immunised. The X^2 - test also did not show any relation. It should however be remembered that immunisation protects children against certain specific diseases only. It can not assure all round health. The basic problem being protein-calorie- malnutrition (PCM).

Table 3.34 Immunisation (Polio) and Infant Health

Infant Health	*POLIO*		
	Not given	*Given*	*Total*
Normal	160 (43.4)	62 (45.6)	222
Poor	160 (43.4)	58 (42.6)	218
Very poor	49 (13.2)	16 (11.8)	65
Total	**369** **(100.0)** **(73.1)**	**136** **(100.0)** **(26.9)**	**505** **(100.0)**

$X^2 = 0.30$, $P > 0.05$ for 2 d.f.

Note: Figures in the parentheses are in percentages

Family Planning and Infant Health

Acceptance of family planning is very low in the study area. Only about 8.5 per cent of the respondents have got sterilised and no one has used or using any spacing method at the time of survey. In the study area, there is not only no influence of acceptance of family planning on child's health, on the other hand, more children of not practising mothers are healthy (45%) than practising mothers (35%) as shown in Table 3.35. The presumption for positive relation between adoption of family planning and infant health is that the adopters have higher socio-economic aspirations than non-adoptors. And thus adopters take better care of their infants. The direct relevance of infant health would arise only when temporary methods are used, which would influence birth interval. This would improve health of the infant. Otherwise, sterilisation of mother by itself need not improve child's health. It might definitely improve health of the mother in due course. This might indirectly improve child's health, through various intermediate variables.

Table 8.85 Practice of Family Planning and Infant Health

Family Planning	*Infant Health*			
	Very poor	*Poor*	*Normal*	*Total*
Practising Family Planning	5 (11.6)	33 (53.5)	15 (34.9)	43 (100.0)
Not practising Fafmily Planning	60 (13.0)	195 (42.2)	20 (45.0)	462 (100.0)
Total	**65**	**218**	**222**	**505**

Note: Figures in the parentheses are in percentages

The reasons stated for using family planning methods are: reduce financial problem of the family (51.2%), preserve health of the mother (18.6%), family property will not be devided (14.7%), improve the health of the children (7.0%), mother's can look after the babies better (2.3%). The reasons expressed for not practising family planning methods are: they like to have more children (40.8%), harmful to mothers health (11.9%), husbands disapproval (5.1%), against religion (2.4%), and mother-in-law disapproves (1.1%).

4

MORBIDITY AND MORTALITY OF INFANTS

In this chapter, morbidity and mortality of infants are discussed. Infant morbidity is a direct measure of infant health, and infant mortality is an indirect measure of infant health.

Morbidity

At the time of survey, illness episode of infants is enquired from the respondents. For the purpose of the present study, illness episode is defined as any ailment suffered for three days or more than three days prior to two months at the time of survey.

From table 4.1 (*See on next page*) it is observed that in the study area, about 40.4 per cent of infants fell ill once or twice. If we look at different age groups of infants, 19.8 per cent fell ill in the age group of 0-2 months, 43.5 per cent in 3-5 months, 43.4 per cent in 6-8 months, and 44.3 per cent in 9-11 months. Thus, the infants who fell ill is almost same in the last three age groups. About 44.9 per cent of infants are normal in health who have not fell ill compare to 42.6 per cent normal who have fell ill showing a marginal differnce of 2.3 percentage points. Infants who have not fell ill have more infants of normal health in all age groups except in 9-11 months compare to infants who fell ill.

Mortality

In India, during 1960s and 1970s infant mortality was very high. In 1980s infant mortality started declining slowly, but still it is considerably high. In this section, infant mortality is analysed by community, occupation, education, age, sex, birth order, respondent's parity, cause of death and treatment, order of infant death and treatment.

Table 4.1 Infant Illness according to Age of the Infant

Age of the Infant	Not fell ill			Fell ill			G-Total
	Normal	Not normal	Total	Normal	Not normal	Total	
0-2	30 (42.2) (52.6)	27 (38.0) (47.4)	57 (80.2) (100.0)	7 (9.9) (50.0)	7 (19.8) (50.0)	14 (100.0) (100.0)	71 (100.0)
3-5	34 (29.6) (52.3)	31 (26.9) (47.7)	65 (56.5) (100.0)	25 (21.8) (50.0)	25 (21.8) (50.0)	50 (43.6) (100.0)	115 (100.0)
6-8	47 (30.9) (54.7)	39 (25.7) (45.3)	86 (56.5) (100.0)	31 (20.4) (47.0)	35 (23.0) (53.0)	66 (43.4) (100.0)	152 (100.0)
9-11	24 (14.4) (25.8)	69 (41.2) (74.2)	93 (55.6) (100.0)	24 (14.4) (32.4)	50 (29.9) (67.6)	74 (44.3) (100.0)	167 (100.0)
Total	**135** **(26.7)** **(44.9)**	**166** **(32.9)** **(55.1)**	**301** **(59.6)** **(100.0)**	**87** **(17.2)** **(42.6)**	**117** **(23.2)** **(37.4)**	**204** **(40.4)** **(100.0)**	**505** **(100.0)**

Note: Figures in the parentheses are in percentages

Community and Infant Death

The average number of infant deaths per woman experienced by community is analysed in table 4.2. The highest average number of infant deaths are observed in the Backward Community (0.57 infant deaths per woman) followed Scheduled Tribes (0.53), Scheduled Castes (0.47), Muslims (0.37) and Forward Community (0.30) respectively (Table 4.2). In the Forward Community the lowest number of infant deaths have occured as expected, because relatively they are economically and socially a better community.

Table 4.2 Distribution of Infant Deaths by Community

Community	*Total number of respondents*	*Total infant deaths*	*Average number of infant deaths*
Forward Community	101	30	0.30
Backward Community	182	103	0.57
Scheduled Castes	78	37	0.47
Scheduled Tribes	77	41	0.53
Muslims	67	25	0.37
Total	**505**	**236**	**0.47**

Respondent's Occupation and Infant Deaths

Occupation is classified only into two groups namely house-wives and labourers. In the study area most of the respondents

Table 4.3 Distribution of Infant Deaths by Respondent's Occupation

Occupation	*Respondents*		*Total*
	Infant death experienced	*Infant death not experienced*	
House-wife	31 (24.4)	96 (75.6)	127 (100)
Labourer	125 (33.1)	253 (66.9)	378 (100)
Total	**156 (30.9)**	**349 (69.1)**	**505 (100)**

$X^2 = 4.1$, $P < 0.01$ for 1 d.f.

Note: Figures in the parentheses are in percentages.

are labourers. A lower proportion of housewives (24.4.%) experienced infant deaths compared to labourers (33.1%) as shown in table 4.3. This may be because of housewife's better economic conditions and she also has more time to look after her children, compared to a labourer in giving breast-milk, feeding supplementary food and looking to personal hygiene, etc. There is a statistically significant association between infant deaths and occupation of the respondents ($X^2 = 4.1$, $P < 0.01$ for 1 d.f.).

Respondent's Distribution of Infant Deaths by Respondent's Education

In the study area, it is found that there is an association between infant deaths experienced by the respondent and education of the respondent. Higher proportion of illiterates (31.6%) compared to literate respondents (23.9%) have experienced infant deaths (Table 4.4.). This is found to be statistically significant. As mentioned earlier, only some respondents are just literate and hence they are classified into two categories.

Table 4.4 Percentage Distribution of Infant Deaths by Respondent's Education

Education	*Respondents*		*Total*
	Infant death experienced	*Infant death not experienced*	
Literate	11 (23.9)	35 (76. 1)	46 (100)
Illiterate	145 (31.6)	314 (68.4)	459 (100)
Total	**156 (30.9)**	**349 (69.1)**	**505 (100)**

$X^2 = 7.16$, $P < 0.01$ for 1 d.f.

Note: Figures in the parentheses are in percentages

Infant Deaths by Age of Respondents

Among all infants, about one third of the respondents (30.9%) have experienced at least one infant death. About 20.2 per cent respondents experienced one infant death, 7.5 per cent two infant deaths, and about 3.2 per cent lost 3 or more infants as shown in table 4.5. As age increases the proportion of infant deaths experienced also increases.

Table 4.5 Distribution of Respondents by Number of Infant Deaths Experienced by Age

Age of the Respondents	*Number of infant deaths experienced by the Respondent*					*Total*
	0	*1*	*2*	*3*	*4+*	
15-19	68 (90.7)	7 (9.3)	—	—	—	75 (100.0)
20-24	153 (80.1)	29 (15.2)	7 (3.7)	1 (0.5)	1 (0.5)	191 (100.0)
25-29	83 (60.1)	41 (29.7)	11 (8.0)	2 (1.4)	1 (0.7)	138 (100.0)
30-34	32 (51.6)	13 (21.0)	12 (19.4)	3 (4.8)	2 (3.2)	62 (100.0)
35-39	10 (33.3)	9 (30.0)	8 26.7)	3 (10.0)	—	30 (100.0)
40-44	3 (33.3)	3 (33.3)	—	—	3 (33.3)	9 (100.0)
Total	**349** **(69.1)**	**102** **(20.2)**	**38** **(7.5)**	**9** **(1.8)**	**7** **(1.4)**	**505** **(100.0)**

Note: Figures in the parentheses are in percentages.

In the age group of 30 to 34, nearly half of the respondents have experienced at least one infant death, and in the age group of 35 years and over, two thirds of the respondents have experienced at least one infant death. About seven respondents have experienced infant deaths of four and above. The maximum number of six infant deaths is experienced by one respondent whose age is only 28 years, followed by only one more woman who experienced five infant deaths whose age is 32 years. Thus, in the study area, infant deaths experienced by the respondents is very high. Death of infants will have great physical strian and mental agony for mothers.

Infant Deaths by Age

Table 4.6 explains the age at death of first infant, second infant, and third and later infants experienced by the respondents. These do not necessarily indicate the order of birth of infants. Among all infant deaths, neonatal mortality (0-28 days, 54.7%) is higher than post-neonatal mortality (29 days and after, 45.3%). Among first infant deaths, the proportion of neo-natal deaths are considerably higher than the second and later infant deaths. In other words, it means the first infant deaths have higher risk after the birth than the subsequent infants. Among the first infant death experienced by the respondents, the proportion of neo-natal deaths (0-28 days) is 57.7 per cent and the proportion of post-neo-natal deaths (after 29 days) is 42.3 per cent. The number of deaths occurred on the first day and in between 2-7 days is 21.8 per cent and 20.5 per cent respectively. The deaths that have occured in the next three weeks are 15.4 per cent. Among the neo-natal deaths 74 per cent (out of 90 neo-natal deaths, 66 deaths are in the first week) have occured during the first week itself and the remaining 26 per cent have occurred in the other three weeks (Fig. 4.1).

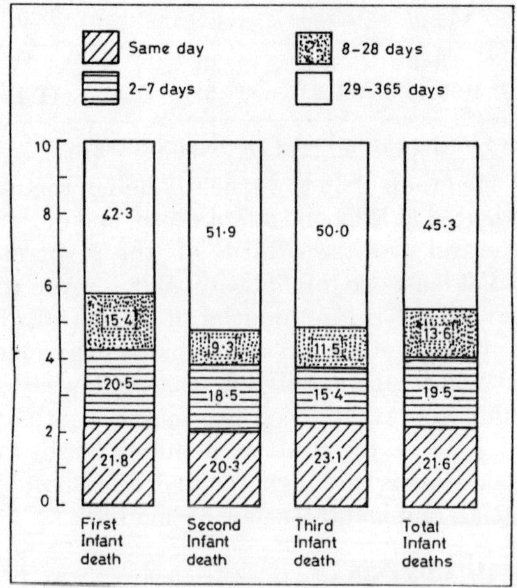

Fig. 4.1. Infant Deaths by Age.

Among the second infant deaths experienced by the respondents, the pattern is slightly different from that of the first. The proportion of neo-natal deaths is slightly lower (4.8%)

than that of post-neo-natal deaths (52%). The number of deaths occured on the first day and in between 2-7 days is 20.3 per cent and 18.5 per cent respectively. Among the neo-natal deaths 80.0 per cent of the deaths (out of 26 neo-natal deaths, 21 deaths are in the first week) have occured in the first week itself (Fig. 4.1).

If we compare the neo-natal and post-neo-natal deaths, those among the first infant deaths, neo-natal deaths are more than post-neo-natal deaths, but among the second, and the third and later infant deaths experienced by the respondents, the proportion of neo-natal and post-neo-natal deaths are almost the same. In other words, it means the first-infant death have higher risk immediately after the birth than the subsequent infants. Probably the reason for this is after experiencing the first infant death, mothers might have been more careful in preventing infant deaths in neo-natal period. The infant deaths that occur in the post-neo-natal period can also be prevented by effective health services, good nutrition intake, health education to mother, etc.

Table 4.6 Infant Deaths by Age

Age at infant death	*First infant death*	*Second infant death*	*Third and later infant deaths*	*Total*
Same day	34 (21.8)	11 (20.3)	6 (23. 1)	51 (21.6)
2-7 days	32 (20.5)	10 (18.5)	4 (15.4)	46 (19.5)
8-28 days	24 (15.4)	5 (9.3)	3 (11.5)	32 (13.6)
Total neo-natal	90 (57.7)	26 (48.1)	13 (50.0)	129 (54.7)
29-365 days	66 (42.3)	28 (51.9)	13 (50.0)	107 (45.3)
Total	**156 (100.0)**	**54 (100.0)**	**26 (100.0)**	**236 (100.0)**

Note: (1) Figures in the parentheses are in percentages.
(2) 349 Respondents who have not experienced infant deaths are excluded in this table.

Sex and Age at Death of Infants

It is interesting to know that in our study it is revealed contrary to general expectation that there is no difference between the proportion of male infant deaths (49.6%) and the proportion of female infant deaths (50.4%) as observed in the table 4.7. But when we analyse the pattern of infant deaths by sex and age at death one can observe a different picture of higher proportion of male infants who died on the same day and also within the same week than the female infants. Then, after one week of survival, it is the female infants that are dying more than male infants. This may be due to biological which is universally observed. On the whole, the association between sex and age at death of infants is not statistically significant ($X^2 = 2.19$, $P > 0.05$ for 3 d.f.).

Table 4.7 Sex and Age at Death of Infant

Age at death of infant	*Sex*		*Total*
	Male	*Female*	
Same day	27 (23.1)	24 (20.2)	51 (21.6)
2-7 days	25 (21.4)	21 (17.6)	46 (19.5)
8-28 days	14 (11.9)	18 (15.1)	32 (13.6)
29 days +	51 (43.6)	56 (47.1)	107 (45.3)
Total	**117 (100.0) (49.6)**	**119 (100.0) (50.4)**	**236 (100.0) (100.0)**

$X^2 = 2.19$, $P > 0.05$ for 3 d.f

Note: Figures in the parentheses are in percentages

Parity of Woman and Infant Deaths

Infant deaths are analysed according to parity of women. Only 12.0 per cent of women with 1 to 3 parity have experienced infant deaths. (Table 4.8). Among women with 4 to 6, and 7 and over parity, 54.1 per cent and 71.4. per cent of women have experienced infant deaths respectively. One can observe that as parity is increasing, infant deaths experienced by women are also increased. This is confirmed by X^2-test also. After third parity if women practice family planning particularly permanent methods (tubectomy or vasectomy) about 77 per cent of infant deaths can be prevented (120 out of 156 of 4th and above parity).

Table 4.8 Infant Deaths by Parity of Women

Parity	*Respondents*		*Total*
	Infant death experienced	*Infant death not experienced*	
1-3	36 (12.0)	263 (88.0)	299 (100.0)
4-6	85 (54.1)	72 (28.6)	157 (100.0)
7+	35 (71.4)	14 (28.6)	49 (100.0)
Total	**156 (30.9)**	**349 (69.1)**	**505 (100.0)**

$X^2 = 127.5$, $P = 0.01$ for 2 d.f.
Note: Figures in the parentheses are in percentages,

Sex and Birth Order of Infant Deaths

Sex and birth order of infant deaths are analysed in table 4.9 (*See on next page*). First birth order, and second birth order deaths of infants are more among male infants than female infants. But the proportion of female infant deaths among third or more birth order are slightly higher than male infant deaths. It seems that the female infants of first and second birth order are better cared, compared to those of third and higher order of female infants. Social problems like dowry may also be partly responsible.

Cause of Infant Death

In the present section for the infant deaths experienced by the respondents, the cause of infant death is enquired into. The

Table 4.9. Sex and Birth Order of Infant Deaths

Birth Order of Infant Deaths	*Sex*		*Total*
	Male	*Female*	
I	43 (36.8)	40 (33.6)	83 (35.2)
2	34 (29. 1)	33 (27.7)	67 (28.4)
3 +	40 (34.1)	46 (38.7)	86 (36.4)
Total	**117** **(100.0)** **(49.6)**	**119** **(100.0)** **(50.4)**	**236** **(100.0)** **(100.0)**

Note: Figures in the parentheses are in percentages.

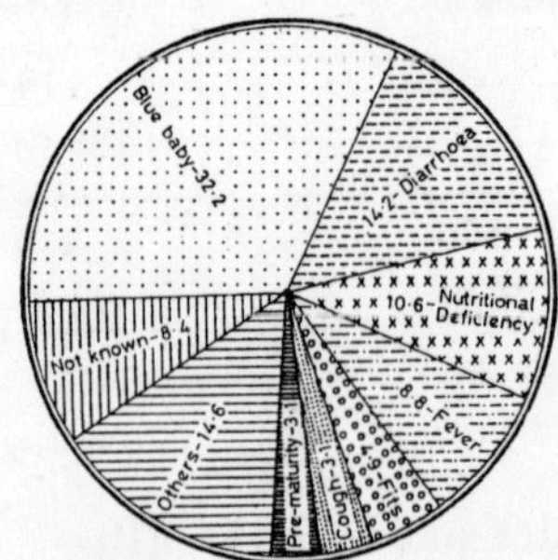

Fig. 4.2 Cause of Infant Deaths

investigators have elicited the most probable cause of death based on the symptoms, conditions and duration of the disease as observed by the respondent at the time of death. This approach is practical and only requires to be intelligently followed. The cause of death based on lay reporting is important in India as most of the deaths are not attended by a trained medical personnel. From the table 4.10, it is observed that the highest proportion of infant deaths occured due to blue baby (32.3%) followed by diarrhoea (14..2%), nutritional deficiency (10.6%), fever (8.8%), fits (4.9%), and others (14.6%). The cause of infant deaths are not known for about 8.4 per cent of infant deaths. Others include rat bite, measles, chicken-pox, ulcers on the body, etc., (Fig. 4.2).

Table 4.10. Infant Deaths by Cause and Treatment Given or Not Given

Cause of Death	*Treatment*		*Total*	*Percentage*
	Given	*Not given*		
Blue baby	9 (12.3)	64 (87.7)	73 (100.0)	32.2
Diarrhoea	11 (34.4)	21 (65.6)	32 (100.0)	14.2
Cough	3 (42.9)	4 (57.1)	7 (100.0)	3.1
Pre-maturity	—	7 (100.0)	7 (100.0)	3.1
Fever	14 (70.0)	6 (30.0)	20 (100.0)	8.8
Nutritional deficiency	5 (20.8)	19 (79.2)	24 (100.0)	10.6
Fits	4 (36.4)	7 (63.6)	11 (100.0)	4.9
Others	10 (30.3)	23 (69.7)	33 (100.0)	14.6
Not known	2 (10.5)	17 (89.5)	19 (100.0)	8.4
Total	**58** **(25.7)**	**168** **(74.3)**	**226** **(100.0)**	**100.0**

Note: (1) Figures in the parentheses are in percentages
(2) Since there was no proper response on cause of death for 10 infant deaths, they are excluded from this table.

Only 25.7 per cent of infants were given treatment before their death. out of these 70.0 per cent infants who died due to fever were given treatment. For coughs, fits and diarrhoea 42.9 per cent, 36.4 per cent, and 34.4 per cent were given treatment respectively. For nutritional difficiency and blue baby, the treatment given is very less, *i.e.*, 20.8 per cent, and 12.3 per cent respectively. The blue baby infant deaths mostly have occured in the first week itself. If proper health care is provided most of these diseases are preventable.

Order of Infant Deaths and Treatment

For the first three infant deaths experienced by the respondents, whether the treatment was given or not is enquired into.

For the first infant death experienced by the respondent, it is observed that 23.7 per cent of the infants were given treatment and the remaining were not given. For the second and third infant deaths, 29.6 per cent and 31.2 per cent of infants were given treatment respectively. In other words, there was a slight improvement in giving treament after experiencing first infant death. This may be due to the fact that after experiencing first infant death, they might have taken a little more care in preventing the subsequent infant deaths.

Table 4.11 Distribution of Infant Deaths by Order and Treatment

Order of Infant Death	*Treatment*		*Total*
	Given	*Not given*	
First Infant Death	37 (23.7)	119 (76.3)	156 (100)
Second Infant Death	16 (29.6)	38 (70.4)	54 (100)
Third Infant Death	5 (31.2)	11 (68.8)	16 (100)
Total	**58** **(25.7)**	**168** **(74.3)**	**226** **(100)**

Note: Figures in the parentheses are in percentages.

5

MULTIVARIATE ANALYSIS OF INFANT HEALTH

In addition to simple descriptive statistics to study infant health discussed earlier we will be using multiple regression analysis in this chapter. Before discussing multiple regression analysis, we will describe different variables used in multiple regression analysis and their means and standard deviations.

Description of Variables

Socio-economic and demographic variables are of interval, ordinal or categorical data. Thirty one variables of these are considered for multiple regression analysis. They are displayed in table 5.1 with variable name, and it's definition.

Table 5.1 Variable Number, Variable Name and It's Definition

Variable number	*Variable name*	*Variable definition*
1	*2*	*3*
V_{01}	Husband's habits	Four habits are classified, *i.e.*, smoking, drinking, playing cards, and chewing tobacco.
V_{02}	Wife's habits	Three habits are classified, *i.e.*, smoking, drinking and chewing tobacco.
V_{03}	Health problems during pregnancy	Health problems during pregnancy are classified into no problems, bleeding, toxemia, systemic diseases, swelling of hands, severe vomiting, B.P., convulsions,

(*Contd....*)

1	*2*	*3*
		hydramnios, headache, giddiness, pain in back and abdomin, weakness, indigestions, acute diarrhoea and others.
V_{04}	Complications in the post-natal period	Complications in the post-natal period are classified into no complications, backache, body pains and weakness, fever, breast pain, over heat, chest pain and giddiness, diarrhoea, stomach discomfort and others.
V_{05}	Health education	Information is collected about the additional food intake at pregnancy and lactation and health check-up during pregnancy and also knowledge about breast milk.
V_{06}	Breast milk	Information elicited on advantages of breast milk.
V_{07}	Services available at health centre	Services regarding treatment, health check-up of mother and child, immunisation, family planning services and communicable diseases enquired.
V_{08}	Breast problems	Information on breast problems are classified as: engorged, abscess, cracked nipple, pain in breast, retracted nipple, redness of the breast, hardness of the nipple and others.
V_{09}	Immunisation	Immunisation regarding six child diseases collected.

(Contd...)

1	*2*	*3*
V_{10}	Practice of family planning	Practice of family planning or not
V_{11}	Morbidity episode	Frequency of illness suffered for three days or more prior to two months at the time of survey.
V_{12}	Adequacy of breast milk	Adequacy of breast milk is classified as less, sufficient, and surplus.
V_{13}	Age of the infant	Infants age in months.
V_{14}	Income	Annual Income of the family.
V_{15}	Education of the respondent	Classified as literates and illiterates only.
V_{16}	Number of living children	Living children of the respondent
V_{17}	Additional food given during pregnancy	Classified as 'No' or 'Yes'
V_{18}	Additional food given during lactation	Classified as 'No' or 'Yes'
V_{19}	Foods avoided during pregnancy	Classified as 'No' or 'Yes'
V_{20}	Foods avoided during lactation.	Classified as 'No' or 'Yes'
V_{21}	Medical check-up during pregnancy	Frequency of medical check-up
V_{22}	Delivery attendant	Classified as mother, mother-in-law, relative, untrained Dai, trained Dai, ANM and doctor.
V_{23}	Bathing per week	Frequency of taking bath in a week.
V_{24}	Mother's height	In centimeters
V_{25}	Mothers weight	In kilograms

(*Contd...*)

1	*2*	*3*
V_{26}	Ideal space between pregnancies	In Years
V_{27}	Infant's attendent	Mother, grand parents, and others.
V_{28}	Infant deaths	Number of infant deaths experienced by the mother
V_{29}	Husband's literacy	Classified as illiterate and literate only
V_{30}	Caste/Religion	Scheduled Caste, Scheduled Tribe, Backward Caste, Muslims, Forward Caste.
V_{31}	Infant health	Classified as 'poor' 'very poor' and 'normal'.

Arithmetic means and standard deviations for 30 variables which are considered for correlation matrix and multivariate regression analysis are given in table 5.2. The values are for coded values.

Table 5.2 Means, standard deviations and range for 30 variables

Variable Number	*Variable Name*	*Mean*	*Standard Deviation*	*Range*
1	*2*	*3*	*4*	*5*
V_{01}	Husband's habits	1.063	0.988	0-4
V_{02}	Wife ' s habits	0.628	0.664	0-3
V_{03}	Health problems during pregnancy	3.291	3.149	0-15
V_{04}	Complications in the post-natal period	0.459	0.750	0-2
V_{05}	Health education	1.200	1.169	0-3
V_{06}	Breast milk (H.E)	1.055	0.998	0-8
V_{07}	Services available at health centre	3.469	1.815	0-5

(Contd...)

1	*2*	*3*	*4*	*5*
V_{08}	Breast problems	0.208	0.712	0-8
V_{09}	Immunisation	0.996	1.208	0-3
V_{10}	Practice of family planning	0.081	0.273	0-1
V_{11}	Morbidity episode	0.778	0.844	0-2
V_{12}	Adequacy of breast milk	1.762	0.675	1-3
V_{13}	Age of supplementary foods started	0.986	0.827	0-2
V_{14}	Income	2,348	1,157	2000-40000
V_{15}	Wife's education	0.091	0.288	0-1
V_{16}	Number of living children	2.699	1.561	1-9
V_{17}	Additional foods given during pregnancy	0.182	0.386	0-1
V_{18}	Additional foods given during lactation	0.079	0.270	0-1
V_{19}	Foods avoided during Pregnancy	1.521	0.500	1-2
V_{20}	Foods avoided during lactation	1.669	0.471	1-2
V_{21}	Medical check-up during pregnancy	1.432	2.181	0-9
V_{22}	Delivery attendent	0.283	0.602	0-2
V_{23}	Bathing per week	1.531	1.291	0-7
V_{24}	Mother's height (c.m)	151.913	20.4	135.0-172.0
V_{25}	Mother's weight (kg)	40.966	5.467	29-60
V_{26}	Ideal space between pregnancies	2.372	1.453	1-5
V_{27}	Infants' attendant	1.192	0.836	0-2
V_{28}	Infant deaths	0.493	0.913	0-9
V_{29}	Husband's education	0.178	0.430	0-1
V_{30}	Caste/Religion	2.653	1.315	1-5
V_{31}	Infant health	2.311	0.687	1-3

Table 5.3 Correlation Matrix

V. No.	V01	V02	V03	V04	V05	V06	V07	V08	V09	V10	V11
V1	1.000										
V2	0.454	1.000									
V3	0.044	0.064	1.000								
V4	0.031	0.110	0.235	1.000							
V5	0.165	0.148	—0.048	—0.017	1.000						
V6	0.086	—0.020	0.066	0.016	0.230	1.000					
V7	—0.139	—0.199	0.039	0.064	0.126	0.142	1.000				
V8	0.007	—0.021	0.190	0.003	—0.029	—0.050	—0.013	1.000			
V9	—0.133	—0.071	0.031	0.000	—0.016	—0.098	0.174	—0.018	1.000		
V10	0.054	0.068	—0.030	—0.002	0.055	0.049	—0.055	—0.025	0.013	1.000	
V11	0.081	0.013	0.213	0.036	—0.021	—0.031	—0.001	0.006	—0.081	—0.025	1.000
V12	0.032	0.050	—0.153	—0.003	0.083	0.202	—0.077	—0.062	0.074	0.073	—0.082
V13	—0.042	0.034	0.025	0.004	—0.032	—0.004	—0.031	0.049	0.117	0.039	—0.030
V14	—0.123	—0.127	—0.002	—0.004	0.066	0.014	0.128	0.062	0.066	0.030	—0.005
V15	—0.132	—0.186	0.007	0.036	0.094	0.051	0.112	—0.043	0.064	0.158	—0.051
V16	0.092	0.010	0.095	0.013	—0.086	—0.035	—0.009	0.096	0.018	0.099	0.049
V17	—0.072	—0.106	—0.077	—0.032	0.016	0.124	0.101	0.050	0.023	0.028	—0.052
V18	—0.123	—0.090	—0.057	—0.043	0.025	0.053	0.066	0.003	0.001	0.007	—0.025
V19	0.154	0.149	—0.059	—0.063	—0.156	—0.094	—0.082	0.004	—0.102	—0.005	0.067
V20	0.130	0.062	—0.018	—0.041	—0.042	—0.282	—0.143	0.058	—0.044	—0.039	0.100
V21	—0.093	—0.168	0.132	0.046	0.164	0.018	0.193	0.004	0.070	0.041	0.077
V22	—0.150	—0.170	0.040	0.037	0.140	0.037	0.127	0.015	0.149	0.029	0.054
V23	—0.034	—0.116	—0.045	0.039	0.112	0.134	—0.063	0.001	0.038	0.021	—0.012
V24	—0.043	0.007	—0.031	—0.029	0.117	0.143	0.079	0.000	0.037	0.106	—0.036
V25	—0.054	—0.048	—0.093	—0.026	0.056	0.076	0.038	0.018	0.005	0.026	—0.035
V26	—0.039	—0.099	—0.039	—0.015	0.090	0.120	0.235	—0.026	0.090	0.034	—0.087
V27	—0.137	—0.189	0.104	0.027	0.103	0.104	0.178	—0.037	0.019	0.018	0.066
V28	0.091	0.130	0.013	0.010	—0.041	—0.124	—0.001	0.024	—0.000	—0.006	0.020
V29	0.238	0.023	—0.011	—0.128	0.056	0.124	0.009	—0.054	0.087	0.025	—0.014
V30	—0.108	—0.061	0.049	0.058	—0.145	—0.147	—0.110	—0.150	—0.049	—0.034	—0.050
V31	—0.064	—0.028	—0.031	—0.259	0.114	0.150	0.048	—0.026	0.042	0.029	—0.114

V12	V13	V14	V15	V16	V17	V18	V19	V20	V21	V22
1.000										
0.155	1.000									
0.079	—0.062	1.000								
0.011	—0.036	0.262	1.000							
—0.248	0.015	—0.005	—0.004	1.000						
0.138	0.023	0.058	0.082	—0.119	1.000					
0.060	0.049	0.000	0.016	—0.056	0.450	1.000				
—0.021	—0.040	—0.099	—0.096	0.105	—0.081	—0.002	1.000			
—0.092	—0.002	—0.000	—0.091	0.028	—0.017	—0.074	0.236	1.000		
0.204	—0.040	0.188	0.244	—0.132	0.133	0.103	—0.136	—0.060	1.000	
—0.098	—0.000	0.134	0.274	—0.106	0.136	0.069	—0.148	—0.009	0.273	1.000
0.011	—0.008	0.103	0.222	—0.057	—0.052	—0.041	—0.039	—0.103	0.135	0.171
0.036	0.027	0.062	0.103	—0.036	0.048	0.020	—0.110	—0.020	0.091	0.142
0.025	0.033	0.142	0.154	—0.053	0.017	0.045	—0.112	—0.011	0.101	0.114
0.072	—0.032	0.065	0089	0.098	0.013	0.001	0.114	0.104	0.114	0.120
0.028	—0.013	0.104	0.125	—0.092	0.082	0.020	—0.021	—0.171	0.174	0.081
—0.062	—0.046	—0.091	—0.073	0.195	—0.070	—0.014	0.003	0.031	—0.041	—0.092
0.006	0.000	0.260	0.481	—0.049	0.145	0.049	—0.153	—0.037	0.261	0.184
—0.013	0.000	0.218	0.179	—0.132	0.170	0.063	—0.198	—0.270	0.141	0.148
0.299	—0.027	0.175	0.158	—0.115	0.034	0.095	—0.233	—0.436	0.028	0.031

V23	V24	V25	V26	V27	V28	V29	V30	V31
1.000								
0.126	1.000							
0.061	0.492	1.000						
0.107	0.060	0.072	1.000					
—0.058	0.042	0.047	0.046	1.000				
—0.024	—0.052	—0.052	—0.080	0.006	1.000			
0.151	0.063	0.130	0.030	0.029	—0.172	1.000		
0.050	0.126	0.154	0.169	0.050	—0.016	0.279	1.000	
0.064	0.063	0.074	0.015	—0.025	—0.205	0.158	0.116	1.000

Note: V—Variable 0.087 < = < 0.114 is significant at 0.05 level.
For n = 505 0.114 < = < 1.000 is significant at 0.01 level

Correlation Matrix

As a prelude to multivariate analysis that follows a correlation matrix is presented in Table 5.3 which shows a bivariate relationship of several variables. It helps us to get a first hand knowledge about the multicolinearity problem in regression analysis that may occur owing to high correlation among the selected variables (usually the factors that have correlation value of more than 0.70 tend to have multicolinearity problem). All the variables in this model reveal that none of them is highly correlated. Data in table 5.3 clearly shows the variables which are significantly related with infant health are:

Complications in the post-natal period, health education, adequacy of breast-milk, income of the family, education of the respondent, number of living children, foods avoided during pregnancy, foods avoided during lactation, infant deaths experienced by the mother, and husband's literacy.

Multiple Regression Analysis (step-wise)

In multiple regression, our analytical model will be additive rather than multiplicative. In additive model, we can see how the addition of one independent variable explains significantly the variation in the dependent variable after controlling for the effect of the proceeding variables. Thus, multiple regression analysis is used to explore the effects of the main independent variables on the dependent variable (infant health).

$$Y = a + b_1 X_1 + b_2 X_2 + \dots\dots\dots\dots\dots\dots + b_n X_n + e$$

Where

Y = the predicted score on the dependent variable

a = is a constant and it is predicted Y score when all independent variables equal to '0' $X_1, X_2 \dots\dots X_n$ are 'n' set of independent variables

b_1 = partial regression co-efficient for X_1 with all other independent variables being controlled.

b_2 = partial regression co-efficient for X_2 with all other independent variables being controlled.

$b_1\, b_2 \dots b_n$ are 'n' partial regression co-efficients

e = is the residual or error term.

In this study, the dependent variable 'infant health' is regressed against 30 variables. The data from the computer analysis has shown that about 46.48 per cent of the variance (R^2) of infant health is explained by all factors taken together.

The multiple regression analysis is shown in table 5.4. The first independent variable entered into multiple regression analysis is "foods avoided during lactation" (X_1). From the table 5.4, one can see that the multiple correlation 'R' is 0.4363 which is nothing but the simple correlation co-efficient between infant health and 'foods avoided during lactation' (shown in column 2). The co-efficient of multiple determination (R^2) revealed that about 19.04 per cent of the variance in the level of infant health is accounted by this independent variable. The standard error of multiple estimate is 1.30 shown in column 5 reveals that nearly 68.00 per cent of the coded values of 'foods avoided during lactation' lie within the range of ± 1.30 points of predicted 'foods avoided during lactation'. In the first step the regression equation is

$$Y = -0.18606 - 1.3349\, X_1$$

Where

X_1 is "foods avoided during lactation'.

The partial regression co-efficient which is negative indicates that there will be depressing effect on infant health. The partial regression co-efficient –1.3349 in the equation indicates decrease in the infant health by every unit change in the variable X_1. The F value for 'b' is significant at 0.01 level.

The second most important variable that entered into the regression analysis is 'complications in the post-natal period (X_2). The multiple correlation co-efficient that obtained between infant health on one side and the two predictor variables *viz.*, 'foods avoided during lactation' (X_1), and 'complications in the post-natal period' (X_2) on the other side is 0.48. The variation explained by these two independent variables put together is about 23.47 per cent ($R^2 = 0.2347$). Out of this, 5.49 per cent of variance is explained by complications in the post-natal period (X_2) and the remaining 17.98 per cent accounted by 'foods avoided during lactation.' It can be seen that by including "complications in the post-natal period the concentration of first independent variable is brought down from 19.03 per cent to 17.98 per cent is due to inter-correlation between the two predictive variables. The regression equation to predict infant health with 'foods avoided during lactation (X_1) and complications in the post-natal period (X_2) as predictive variables is

$$Y = -0.5697 - 1.2610\, X_1 - 0.2562\, X_2$$

The partial regression co-efficients –1.2610 and –0.2562 in the above equation indicate that the level of infant health would change by –1.2610 and –0.2562 points for every unit increase in X_1, X_2 respectively. Both these partial regression co-efficients are significant at 0.01 level.

The next important independent variable that entered in the third step of the multiple regression analysis is "adequacy of breast milk (X_3)" The multiple correlation co-efficient 'R' is equal to 0.5182 is the combined association with the three independent variables X_1, X_2 and X_3 with that of dependent variable 'infant health'. The value of R^2 equal to 0.2685 disclosed that 26.85 per cent is explained by the three independent variables. Out of this, 15.74. per cent, 5.39 per cent, and 5.72 per cent is accounted for X_1, X_2 and X_3 independent variables respectively. The regression equation at the end of the third step is :

$$Y = -0.8569 - 1.1043\, X_1 - 0.2518\, X_2 + 0.2096\, X_3$$

Where

X_1, X_2 and X_3 are prediction variables.

This equation explain that the partial regression coefficient indicated in the equation that the change in infant health is by –1.1043, –0.2518 and 0.2096 units for every unit increase in foods avoided during lactation, complications in the post-natal period, adequacy of brest milk respectively. The three partial regression coefficients are significant at 0.01 level.

In the fourth step the variable entered is "services available at health centre (X_4)". The multiple correlation co-efficient obtained between the infant health on one side and the other four independent variables X_1, X_2, X_3 and X_4 is 0.5461. The value of R^2 equal to 0.2982 disclosed that about 29.82 per cent of variance is explained by the four independent variables mentioned above. Out of this total per cent of variation explained, 17.22 per cent, 5.23 per cent, 6.51 per cent and 0.86 per cent is accounted for X_1, X_2, X_3 and X_4 independent variables respectively. The regression equation at the end of the fourth step is:

$$Y = -0.3015 - 1.2084\,X_1 - 0.2440\,X_2 + 0.2387\,X_3 + 0.5172\,X_4$$

Where

X_1, X_2, X_3 and X_4 are predictive variables.

In the fifth step, the independent variable that entered is number of infant deaths experienced by mother. The value of $R^2 = 0.3262$ disclosed that about 32.62 per cent of variance is explained by the five independent variables. Out of this 32.62 per cent of variation explained, 16.77 per cent, 4.71 per cent, 6.84 per cent, 0.84 per cent, 3.46 per cent is accounted for X_1, X_2, X_3, X_4 and X_5 independent variables respectively.

The regression equation at the end of fifth step is X_4

$$Y = -0.0002 - 1.1766X_1 - 0.2199X_2 + 0.2508X_3 + 0.5023X_4 - 0.0084X_5$$

In the sixth step, the variable that entered is 'annual family income' (X_6). The value of R^2 equal to 0.3494 disclosed that about 34.94 per cent of variance is explained by the six independent variables. And these six X_1, X_2, X_3, X_4, X_5 and X_6 independent variables are accounted to 16.19 per cent, 4.54 per cent, 7.14 per cent, 0.82 per cent, 3.57 per cent 2.68 per cent respectively. The regression equation at the end of sixth step is:

$$Y = -1.0286 - 1.1362\,X_1 - 0.2116\,X_2 + 0.2618\,X_3 + 0.4957\,X_4.\ 0.0086\,X_5 + 0.0704\,X_6.$$

In the seventh step, the variable that entered is 'foods avoided during pregnancy (X_7). The value of R^2 is equal to 0.3678 disclosed that about 36.78 per cent of variance is explained by seven independent variables. Tire regression equation at the end of the seventh step is:

$$Y = -0.4993 - 1.1095\,X_1 - 0.1943\,X_2 + 0.2438\,X_3 + 0.5154\,X_4 - 0.0082\,X_5 + 0.0702\,X_6 - 0.1105\,X_7$$

The variable that entered in the eigth step is 'number of living children' (X_8). About 36.78 per cent of variation is explained by the eight indipendent variables. The equation in this step is:

$$Y = 0.9160 - 1.0429\,X_1 - 0.2103\,X_2 + 0.2723\,X_3 + 0.4 - 896\,X_4 - 0.0082\,X_5 + 0.0640\,X_6 - 0.1200\,X_7 - 0.6932\,X_8$$

The variable that entered in the ninth step is 'wife's literacy' (X_9). The per cent of variation explained by all these nine variables is 39.76 per cent. The equation in the nineth step is:

$$Y = -0.2285 - 1.0285\,X_1 - 0.2090\,X_2 + 0.2666\,X_3 + 0.4882\,X_4 - .0.0080\,X_5 + 0.0665\,X_6 - 0.1152\,X_7 - 0.6861\,X_8 + 0.5789\,X_9$$

The variation explained by the remaining 21 variables is about 6.72 per cent only.

On the basis of this study, step-wise regression model showed that out of 30 predictors, nine are important predictors of variation in infant health with that order of importance. Thus, the predictors are food avoided during lactation, complications in the post-natal period, adequacy of breast-milk, services available at health centre, number of infant deaths experienced by the mother, annual family income, food avoided during pregnancy, total number of living children and wife's literacy. These variables are the best-set of indicators related with infant health and they need special consideration while framing policies on infant health.

Table 5.4 Multiple Regression Analysis (Step-wise)

S. No.	Predictor variable entered in each step	Multiple correlation (R)	R^2	Standard error of multiple estimate	F-value (d.f.) and level of significance	B-co-efficient (or) 'b' partial Regression co-efficient	F-falue for 'B' and level of significance	Constant	B-beta co-efficient	Simple correlation coefficient	Variance in the dependent variable explained by each independent variable	% of variance
1	2	3	4	5	6	7	8	9	10	11	12	13
1.	Foods avoided during lactation (V_{20})	0.4363	0.1904	1.30	118.3 (1,503)	–1.33487	118.3	–0.18606	–0.4365	–0.436	0.1903	19.03
2.	Complication in the post-natal period (V_4)	0.4844	0.2347	1.26	77.0 (2,502)	–0.25623 –0.26095	29.0 110.0	–0.56970	–0.2118 –0.4123	–0.259 –0.436	0.0549 0.1798	5.49 17.98
3.	Adequacy of breast milk (V_{12})	0.5182	0.2685	1.24	61.3 (3,501)	0.20960 –0.25182 –1.10434	23.2 29.3 81.8	–0.85685	0.1911 –0.2081 –0.3610	0.299 –0.295 –0.436	0.0572 0.0539 0.1574	5.72 5.39 15.74
4.	Services Available at Health centre (V_7)	0.5461	0.2982	1.21	53.1 (4,500)	0.51722 0.23871 –0.24396 –1.20844	21.2 30.6 28.5 98.4	–0.30153	0.1791 0.2176 –0.2016 –0.3950	0.048 0.299 –0.259 –0.436	0.0086 0.0651 0.0523 0.1722	0.86 6.51 5.23 17.22
5.	Number of infant deaths experienced by the mother (V_{28})	0.5711	0.3262	1.19	43.3 (5,499)	–0.00835 0.50232 0.25084 –0.21993 –1.17656	20.7 20.8 35.0 23.8 96.6	–0.00019	–0.1690 0.1740 0.2286 –0.1818 –0.3846	–0.205 0.048 –0.299 –0.259 –0.436	0.0346 0.0084 0.0684 0.0471 0.1677	3.46 0.84 6.84 4.71 16.77

1	*2*	*3*	*4*	*5*	*6*	*7*	*8*	*9*	*10*	*11*	*12*	*13*
6.	Annual Family income (V_{14})	0.5911	0.3494	1.17	44.6	0.07036	17.7	–1.02859	0.1531	0.175	0.0268	2.68
					(6,498)	–0.00859	22.6		–0.1739	–0.205	0.0357	3.57
						0.49574	20.9		0.1717	0.048	0.0082	0.82
						0.26183	39.2		0.2387	0.299	0.0714	7.14
						–0.21163	22.7		–0.1749	–0.259	0.0454	4.54
						–1.13620	92.5		–03714	–0.436	0.1619	16.19
7.	Foods avoided during pregnancy (V_{19})	0.6065	0.3678	1.16	41.3	–0.11052	14.5	–0.49930	–0.1390	–0.233	0.0324	3.24
					(7,497)	0.07021	18.1		0.1528	0.175	0.0267	2.67
						–0.00816	20.9		–0.1652	–0.205	0.0339	3.39
						0.51537	23.1		0.1785	0.048	0.0086	0.86
						0.24377	34.5		0.2222	0.299	0.0664	6.64
						–0.19427	19.4		–0.1606	–0.259	0.0416	4.16
						–0.10951	90.3		–0.3267	–0.436	0.1582	15.82
8.	Total number of living children (V_{13})	0.6208	0.3054	1.14	38.9	–0.69315	14.2	0.19602	–0.1384	–0.115	0.0159	1.59
					(8,496)	–0.12003	17.4		–0.1510	–0.233	0.0352	3.52
						0.06402	15.3		0.1393	0.175	0.0244	2.44
						–0.00815	21.4		–0.1650	–0.205	0.0330	3.38
						0.48961	21.4		0.1696	0.048	0.0081	0.81
						0.27225	42.7		0.2482	0.299	0.0742	7.42
						–0.21028	23.2		–0.1738	–0.259	0.0451	4.51
						–0.04292	80.0		–0.3409	–0.436	0.1487	14.84
9.	Wife's literacy (V_{15})	0.6305	0.3976	1.13	36.3	0.57894	10.0	–0.22850	0.1109	0.158	0.0175	1.75
					(9,495)	–0.68607	14.2		–0.1370	–0.115	0.0157	1.57
						–0.11520	16.3		–0.1449	–0.233	0.0338	3.38
						0.06650	16.8		0.1447	0.175	0.0253	2.53
						–0.00796	20.7		–0.1611	–0.205	0.0330	3.30
						0.48823	21.6		0.1691	0.048	0.0081	0.81
						0.26663	41.6		0.2430	0.299	0.0727	7.27
						–0.20896	23.3		–0.1727	–0.259	0.0448	4.48
						–1.02846	79.1		–0.3362	–0.436	0.1467	14.67

6

SUMMARY AND CONCLUSIONS

Introduction

Children are the most vulnerable group of the population. In India, infants (under one year of age) constitute 2.5 per cent of the total population. The total number of babies born in India is the highest in the world. Many infants die before reaching their first birth day. Among the total infant deaths in the world, India's share of infant deaths is 27.6 per cent followed by China (9.3%) and Bangladesh (5.0%). It is only 3.0 per cent for the more developed countries in 1975-80 (U.N. 1984: 106). Hence, this study focuses on infant health from various angles like nutrition, socio-economic factors, demographic factors, health education, illness episode, utilisation of health services, etc.

This study is conducted in rural area of Kuppam taluq of Chittoor district in Andhra Pradesh. This Kuppam taluq is the most backward area of Chittoor district. In this study, the sampling unit is a married woman with an infant child. The total sample size covered is 505. In this study, infant health is measured in terms of nutritional status. Accordingly, infant's health is classified as 'normal health', 'poor health' and 'very poor health'. Reference values calculated by W.H.O. from the median reference value recommended is taken as standard of reference for the present study.

Socio-economic and Demographic Background of the Respondent

The socio-economic differentials among the population are studied. About housing in the study area, out of 505 respondents 42.6 per cent are living in ' Huts', 38.6 per cent are in 'Kutcha' houses and the remaining 18.8 per cent of the respondents are living in 'Pucca' houses. Walls of mud and roofs of thatch (grass) are predominant in the study area.

The average size of the household in the study area is 7.6 persons. The range of the household' size is 3 to 35 members. Among different communities, the average size of the household is the highest in the Forward Community (9.5) followed by Muslims (7.7), Backward Community (7.1), Scheduled Tribe (6.6), and Scheduled Caste (6.4). In the study area, education among the respondents and their husbands is very low (husbands 20%; wives 9%) . Among the different communities (Forward Community, Backward Community, Scheduled Castes, Scheduled Tribes, and Muslims) Backward Community constitute the major group (36.0%). Occupations of the husbands of the respondents, the highest proportion belongs to agricultural labourers (60.1%), followed by cultivators (21.0%), cultivators cum agricultural labourers (11.6%), services and business each 3.0 per cent and the remaining belong to artisans, namely, washermen and pot makers (1.3%). Agricultural labourers are highest among Scheduled Tribes (98.7%) followed by Scheduled Castes (87.1%), Muslims (59.7%), Backward Community (49.4%) and Forward Community (28.3%). In the study area, work participation among respondents is also very high. Even among Forward Community the proportion of workers is high. Most *of* them are working hard in agricultural field.

The average annual family income of the respondent is Rs. 2,280. Most of the families (81%) have low and very low income (less than Rs. 4000). Among different communities, Scheduled Castes and Scheduled Tribes and Muslims have less income compared to the families of Forward Community and Backward Community families.

About age distribution of the respondents, eighty per cent of the respondents are young (less than or equal to 29 years), and 18.2 per cent belong to middle age group (30-39 years), the remaining 1.8 per cent are old women (40-49 years). Considerable proportion (14.9%) is of very young women (15-19 age group). Further reduction of women with an infant child in this age group of 15-19 is very essential for better health of children.

The mean age at marriage for all communities is 14.75 years. The highest mean age at marriage is observed in

Forward Community (15.3 years) and the lowest is observed in Backward Community (14.23 years). The highest proportion of the respondents (55.4%) married between 11 to 15 years and 5.7 per cent of the respondents married at 10 years of age or below. Only 22.5 per cent of respondents married at age 18 years and above.

About fertility, 24.8 per cent of the respondents have one living child and 27.9 per cent have two living children and the remaining respondents (47.3%) have three and more than three children. The average number of live births and living children is 3.21, and 2.71 per woman respectively. This indicates that on an average there is a loss of one child for every two women reflecting a heavey loss of children and low child health.

Determinants of Infant Health

The determinants of infant's health are complex. However, an attempt is made to identify factors influencing infant health. The demographic characteristics of the infant, socio-economic and demographic background of the mother, food and nutrition of the mother and child, health of the mother, feeding pattern, health services and family planning, morbidity and mortality of infants are analysed.

Demographic Characteristics of the Infant

The main demographic characteristics of the infant that have impact on infant health are age, sex, weight and birth order, etc. Measurement of weight-for-age is the method of choice for the assessment and surveillance of the child's state of health. Among boys, progressive increase in mean weight is noted upto 8 months and then declines. Among girls mean weight gradually increases with age without any set back. At each age, the mean weight of the girls is lower than the mean weight of the boys as is universally observed.

In the study area, among the total infants, the proportion of 'normals' are 43.9 per cent, 43.2 per cent are of 'poor health' and the remaining 12.9 per cent are of very poor health'. The proportion of 'normals' among boys and girls are 44.6 per cent and 43.3 per cent respectively and this difference is not statistically significant. The proportion of very poor health in boys and girls is 13.2 per cent and 12.6 per cent respectively. It is found that among boys the percentage of 'normals' increases from 47.7 per cent in the age group of 0-2 months to 53 per cent in 6-8 months, then declines to 29.9 per cent in 9-11 months of age. Among girls, the proportion of the healthy, declines continuously from 59.3 per cent in 0-2 months to 28 per cent in the age group of 9-11 months. Thus, the pattern is different between boys and girls. After eight months both among boys and girls there is a steep decline of normals which again reflects malnutrition among older babies. Another interesting observation is the proportion of healthy children is considerably higher in the age group of 0-2 among girls (59%) than boys (48%). But, on the whole there is no difference between boys and girls.

Birth order has got influence on infant health. Among male infants of 3rd or lower order, about 48.7 per cent of infants are healthy, whereas, infants whose birth order is more than 3, only 39.2 per cent of infants are healthy. Thus, normals are more among infants of lower birth order compared to infants of higher birth order.

Socio-economic Background of the Mother

Many socio-economic variables have positive influence on infant health. About father's and mother's education, it is observed that in the present study, infant health and mother's literacy level are positively correlated; about 56.5 per cent of literate mothers have infants of normal health in contrast to 42.7 per cent of illiterate mothers. The proportion of 'poor health and very poor health' infants are higher among illiterate mothers compare to literate mothers. Similar trend is observed with educational level of fathers except that among the infants of 'poor health'. In our study, mother's level of education does show better influence than that of fathers, while about 56.5 per cent of literate mothers have healthy children, the corresponding proportion for father's is about 50 per cent. The gap between literate and illiterate mothers having healthy children is about 14 percentage points as against eight percentage points for fathers. This clearly indicates that more the mothers are literate the more infants are healthy.

The mothers occupational status is classified into two categories namely, worker and non-worker. In this study, about 75.4 per cent of mothers are workers, 24.6 per cent of mothers are non-workers. The health of the infant is almost similar whether their mothers are workers or non-workers.

If we look infant health by community-wise, the highest proportion of normal infants are in the Forward Community (52.4%), followed by infants of Scheduled Tribes (44.2%), Backward Community (42.3%) and infants of the Muslim Community (41.8%). The least proportion of normal infants is found among Scheduled Castes (38.5%). This is because, the Scheduled Caste Community is economically and socially lowest among all the communities. After Forward Community, infants in Scheduled Tribes have better health than the infants of other three communities. The possible reason may be that among Scheduled Tribes, they have less taboos on foods during pregnancy and lactation time and also they used to take raw food rich in nutrition though not rich in cost. These habits will have it's positive effect on infant health, and it appears to be true in the study area.

About family annual income and infant health, it is observed that with the increase in the level of family income, the proportion of healthy infants progressively increases from 38 per cent in the income level of below Rs. 2,000 to about 57 per cent in the income level of Rs. 6,000 and above. The association between income and infant health is positively related.

In this study, the proportion of healthy children is slightly more in joint families (45.2%) comparatively than in nuclear families (42.3%). However, the difference between family type and infant health is not statistically significant.

Demographic Characteristics of the Mothers

Age of the mother has it's effect on the health of the infant. Young mothers (under 29 years) have healthier infants than that of old mothers (30 years and above,). There is a decline in the level of infant health if the mother's age is more than 30 years and above. This may be due to deteriorating nutritional status of mothers, repeated pregnancies and also due to poor economic conditions. In this study, it is found that there is no relationship between age at marriage and infant health. it seems besides age at marriage on motherhood, there are other more important determinants of infant health at least in this study area.

About one third of the mothers have experienced at least one infant death. The health status of infants whose mothers have not experienced infant deaths is slightly better compared to the infants whose mothers have experienced infant death.

Food and Nutrition of the Mother and Infant

In the study area, due to poor economic conditions pregnant women are not taking additional foods in sufficient quantity during pregnancy and lactation. Only 18.2 per cent of women have taken additional foods during pregnancy. They are not even taking sufficient quantity of food during normal time when they are not pregnant. In the study area, it is found that there is no association between additional foods taken during pregnancy and infant health.

About 8.3 per cent have taken additional foods during lactation. There is no difference in the health status of infants between those who have taken and not taken additional foods during the lactation period.

Among women who avoided certain foods during pregnancy, 41.6 per cent of their infants are normal in health, whereas 46.1 per cent of infants are normal in health among the mothers who did not avoid any food during pregnancy period. This shows significant influence on infant health of avoiding nutritious food during pregnancy due to ignorance or superstition.

Certain foods are avoided during lactation. The reasons for avoiding these foods are due to the belief that the mother and also the child will suffer from cold, cough and fever, some women also said that, infants will not survive if these foods are consumed. About one third of women have avoided certain foods during lactation. The proportion of healthy children are less for those women who avoided certain foods during lactation compared to women who have not avoided those foods.

Feeding pattern of infants in first three days has no influence on infant health. In this study, most of the mothers think that breast milk is enough for the infants at least for one year. The respondents were enquired about their perception of the adequacy of breast milk for their infants. It is observed that about 61.4 per cent of the total respondents said they have sufficient and surplus milk. The remaining 38.6 per cent said that they have inadequate milk. The proportion of normal infants are more with the mothers of sufficient and surplus milk compare to mothers of inadequate milk. However, older infants will not be assured of normal health even if their mothers have sufficient and even surplus milk. This emphasises the necessity of supplementary food. In the study area supplementary foods are not properly given. Only about 44 per cent of the infants are given supplementary foods. If for any reason mothers have no breast milk, then only the infants are fed with animal's milk. Only about 57 per cent of the infants are given supplementary foods at age six months and over. Moreover, the respondents have little knowledge about the quantity and quality of the supplementary foods to be given to infants. When the elders are eating in the family, they just provide the same foods to the infants, and they do not bother much whether the infants were fed or not properly. There is no significant relationship between supplementary foods given and infant health.

The average weight and height of a woman in the study area is 40.97 kilogrames and 151.9 centimeters respectively. There is no association between weight of a woman and infant health and also height of a woman and infant health.

Health of the Mother

Health of the mother is discussed in terms of complications during pregnancy and lactation. The most predominant health problems during pregnancy are pain in back and in abdomin (45.5%) followed by weakness (45%), giddiness (42.6%), swelling of hands (38.2%), indigestion (34.5%), severe vomiting (30.5%), bleeding (18.0%), and hydromniosis (12.9%) and only a few respondents had toximia (2.6%). Among the said above health problems, only hydromniosis has shown significant influence on infant health.

The Post-natal complications that have been reported in the study by the respondents are: body pains, backache, weakness, breast pain, diarrhoea, stomach discomfort, chest-pain, etc. Women who have not suffered have more normal infants (45.8%) compared to the women who have suffered from one or two post-natal complications (39.7%).

Health Services

Health services have greater influence on infant health. In a study area, most of the deliveries are conducted at home. Among the infants delivered at home, about 43.9 per cent of the infants are healthy compared to 44.9 per cent of infants who were delivered in hospital, showing no difference in the health of the infants with the place of delivery conducted whether at home or in hospital.

About medical check-up during pregnancy, 44.9 per cent of the respondents had medical check-up for at least once. Mothers who had medical check-up during pregnancy at least once have 44.1 per cent of the infants healthy as aginst 43.9 per cent of the infants whose mothers did not have medical check-up revealing no association between the two. But, 44.5 per cent of infants are normal whose mothers have medical check-up three and more times, compare to about 39 per cent of infants normal whose mothers have medical check-up only once. Thus, medical check-up during pregnancy has influence on infant health only when they have medical check-up regularly.

Immunisation is very essential to prevent certain diseases of children, namely, tuberculosis, diphtheria, purtosis, tetanus, polio and measels. In the present study, there is no significant difference of normal infants between those immunisation received or not received. Immunisation just protects children against certain specific diseases only. It cannot assure alround health. The basic problem is protein-calorie malnutrition.

Family planning practice is very low in the study area. Only about 8.5 per cent of the respondents have got sterilised and no one has used any spacing method at the time of survey. But in the study area, it has not shown any influence on infant health. The direct relevance of infant health would arise only when temporary methods are used which would influence birth interval. This would improve the health of the infant, otherwise sterilisation of mother by itself need not imporve infant health. It might definitely improve the health of the mother. In due course this might directly improve infants health through various intermediate variables.

Morbidity and Mortality of Infants

Infant morbidity is a direct measure of infant health, and infant mortality is an indirect measure of infant health. At the time of survey, illness episode is enquired among infants during the last two months period. The proportion of infants that fell ill once or twice is 40.4 per cent. About the health of the infant and illness episode about 44.9 per cent of infants are normal who have not fell ill compare to 42.6 per cent normal who have fell ill showing a marginal difference of 2.3 percentage points.

In the study area, 30.9 per cent of respondents have experienced at least one infant death. Community-wise average number of infant deaths experienced per woman is found to be lowest in the Forward Community because relatively they are economically and socially a better community compare to other communities.

Higher proportion of illiterates (32.0%) compare to literate respondents (23.9%) have experienced infant deaths.

A lower proportion of housewives (24.4%) experienced infant deaths compared to labourers (33.1%). This may be because of housewife's better economic conditions and she also has more time to look after her children compare to a labourer in giving breastmilk, feeding supplementary food, looking to personal hygiene, etc. As age of the respondents increases the proportion of infant deaths experienced also increases. In the age group 30-34, nearly half of the respondents have experienced at least one infant death, and in the age group of 35 years and above, two thirds of the respondents have experienced at least one infant death. Thus, infant deaths experienced by the respondents are very high.

If we compare the neo-natal and post-neo-natal deaths according to order of infant deaths, those among the first infant deaths, neo-natal deaths are more than the post-neo-natal deaths, but among the second and the third and later infant deaths experienced by the respondents, the proportion of neo-natal and post-neo-natal deaths is almost the same. In other words, it means the first infant deaths have higher risk immediately after the birth than the subsequent infants. Probably, the reason for this is after experiencing first infant death, mother's might have been a little careful in preventing infants deaths in the neo-natal period.

Out of the total infant deaths, the proportion of male and female infant deaths is almost same. In the first week male infants have died more compared to female infants, again after one month of survival the female infants died more compared to male infants. This may be mainly due to biological which is universely observed.

In the study area, as parity is increasing, infant deaths experienced by the women are also increased. After third parity if women practice family planning particularly permanent methods (tubectomy or vasectomy) about 77 per cent of infant deaths can be prevented.

About birth order, among first and second birth order of infant deaths, male infant deaths are more than female infant deaths. But, among third or later birth order, female infant deaths are more than male infant deaths. It seems that the female infants of first and second birth order of infants are better cared compared to the birth of third and higher order of births of infants. Social problems like dowry may also be partly responsible.

The cause of infant death is enquired into. The highest proportion of infant deaths are occurred due to blue baby (32.3%) followed by diarrhoea (14.2%), nutritional deficiency (10.6%), fever (8.8%), fits (4.9%), and others (12.8%). Only 25.7 per cent of infants were given treatment (medical attention) before their death. For the first infant deaths, 23.7 per cent of the infants were given treatment and the remaining were not given. For the second and third infant deaths, 29.6 per cent and 31.2 per cent of infants were given treatment respectively, the remaining were not at all given. Thus, there was a slight improvement in giving treatment after experiencing first infant death.

Multivariate Analysis

In addition to simple discriptive statistics, multiple regression analysis is also utilised. In this analytical model we can see how the addition of one independent variable explains significantly the variation in dependent variable after controlling for the effect of the preceding variable. Thus, multiple regression analysis is used to explore the effects of the main independent variables on the dependent variable. The regression model is

$$Y = a + b_1x_1 + b_2x_2 + - + b_nx_n + e.$$

In this study, the dependent variable 'infant health' is regressed against 30 variables. The data from the computer analysis showed that about 46.48 per cent of the variance (R^2) of infant health is explained by all factors taken together.

On the basis of this study, step-wise regression model showed that out of 30 predictors, nine are important predictors of variation in infant health. The nine predictors entered into multiple regression analysis in the order of importance are foods avoided during lactation, complications in the post-natal period, adequacy of breast milk, services available at health centre, number of infant deaths experienced by the mother, annual family income, foods avoided during pregnancy, total number of living children, wife's literacy. The per cent of variation explained by all these nine variables is 39.76 per cent. These variables are the best set of indicators related with infant health and they need special consideration while framing the policies on infant health.

Recommendations

In order to tackle the problem of low infant health, it is essential to assess and monitor it's level in different parts of the country, to better understand the distinct causes of low infant health. In the study area, majority of infants are not healthy. To make them healthy, it is very essential to provide better nutrition to mother and infant. Health education must be provided to pregnant and lactating women about adquacy of food. Food taboos are many. Efforts should be made to remove them.

One of the causes for low level of infant health is prolonged breast-feeding with delayed introduction of poor quality supplements. Hence, efforts must be made to educate women to initiate breast-feeding immediately after birth and it can be continued. At the same time, emphasis must be laid on proper supply of supplementary solid foods to infants at the right time during the first year of life (after five or six months).

In view of the fact that most of the deliveries conducted at home by untrained persons, attention should be paid to identification and to involvement of expectent mothers. They must be educated for proper place of delivery. This will help in reducing post-natal complications.

Anaemia is also common among women in reproductive age and it is 60 to 70 per cent in India. Regular distribution of iron and folic tablets is essential. Treatment of minor ailments for both mother and infant would greatly help in achieving full potential of growth in infants.

Prevention of infant deaths is one of the essential component to improve infant health. So health services must be utilised properly and effectively. This can be achieved by regular ante-natal check-up, and also infants health care at primary health centres, sub-centres, and anganwadi centres. It will also identify at-risk mothers and would enable the mothers to decide the place of delivery well in advance.

Income has influence on infant health. Income generating activities be evaluated in rural areas to improve the economic status of the families. This will help in improving infant health through many variables.

Female literacy is very low in the study area. It has to be improved to have a healthy child. Imparting health education to mothers regarding proper infant-feeding practices, additional food required during pregnancy and lactation, on-set and duration of breast-feeding, food taboos, etc., is easier if mothers are literate.

Very few respondents are practising family planning methods, that too permanent methods, hence, spacing methods must be vigorously encouraged.

Immunisation must be given effectively. Incomplete immunisation is as good as not being immunised. It has been observed that the immunisation coverage is generally good for the first dose of vaccines, but gradually for subsequent doses, the number of beneficiaries decreases.

This has to be taken care by follow up activities. A system of immunisation cards should be introduced. The drop-out rate should also be reduced by involving the village heads.

The available data are not sufficient to adequately assess health services and infant health. For this purpose, detailed information is required on type and extent of health services available in the community and their utilisation by the community. Adequate referral and provision of remedial services must be provided to help mother and child.

BIBLIOGRAPHY

Aaby, P., Bukh, J., Lisse, I.M., and Smites, A.J. 1983. "Measles Mortality, State of Nutrition, and Family Structure: A Community Study from Guinea-Bissau", *Journal of Infectious Diseases* 147 (4), April, 1983.

Abbott Laboratories, Ross Division. 1978. *The Volume of Human Milk Produced by Malnourished Mother,* Columbus, Ohi: Abott Laboratories.

Abel, R. 1985. "Delayed Starting of Breast-feeding by Rural Indian Mothers", *Journal of Tropical Paediatrics* 31(4), August 1985.

Ahamad, M.M., Khuda, B. 1984. "Breast-feeding in Developing-Countries: Some Evidences", *Journal of Family Welfare* 31(1).

Ahmed, W., Behein, F., et al. 1981. "Female infant in Egypt: Mortality and Child Care, "*Population Sciences* 1(2).

Anne, R. Pebly 1986. "Birth Spacing and Child Survival", *International Family Planning Perspectives* 12(3).

Anonymous, 1984: "Blocking the Energy Drain", *World Health* October, 1984.

Anrudh, K. Jain. 1988. "Determinants of Regional Variations in Infant Mortality in Rural India", *Infant Mortality in India: Differentials and Determinants,* Ed. Anrudh, K. Jain., and Pravin Visaria. New Delhi: Sage Publications.

Anrudh, K. Jain, and Pravin Visaria. 1988. "Infant Mortality in India, An Overview". Infant Mortality in India: Differentials and Determinants, Ed. Anrudh, K. Jain., and Pravin Visaria. New Delhi: Sage Publications.

Arun Chopdar., Samal, N.C. 1979. "Nutritional Status of Pre-school Children at Subedga", Indian Journal of Paediatrics 46(374).

At Burtan, M.H. 1986-87. "Attitudes and Practice of Kuwaiti Women Toward Breast-feeding", Journal of Bio-social Sciences 7(2).

Atalah, E., Bustos, P., Ruz, M., Hurtado, C., Masson, L., Urteaga, C., Castanos, M., Codoy, R., Oliver, H. , and Araya, J. 1980. "Relationship Between Mother's Nutritional Status, Breast-feeding and Infant Growth (SPA Summary in Eng.)", Revista Chilena de Paediatria 51(3).

Bahe, L. 1979. "Some Aspects of Infant Rearing Practices and Beliefs in Tribal Inhabitants of Himachal Pradesh", Indian Paediatrics 16(4).

Bansal, R.D., Ghosh, B.N., et al. 1973. "Infant Feeding and Weaning Practices at Simla-Hills, Himachal Pradesh", Indian Journal of Medical Research 61(12).

Belavady, B. 1979. "Dietary Supplementation and Improvements in the Lactation Performance of Indian Women", Maternal Nutrition During Pregnancy and Lactation: A Nestle Foundation Workshop, Ed. Aebi, H., and Whitehead, R. Switzerland: Luty Lansanne, (Nestle Foundation Publication Series No. 1).

Bengoa, J.M. 1970. "Recent Trends in the Public Health Aspects of Protein-calorie Malnutrition", *WHO Chronicle* 24.

Berthet, E. 1984. "A Possible Goal by the Year 2000: Reducing Infant Mortality by One Half in Third World Countries", *Hygie* 3(2).

Bhandari, B. , Nagori, G., Mandowra, S.L. 1981. "Nutritional and Immunisation Status of Children in an ICDS Block", *Indian Paediatrics* 18, March 1981.

Biering - Sorensen, F. , Hilden, J.,Hiring Sorensen, K. 1983. "Breast-feeding and Infant Health in Capenhagen 1941-1972," Danish Medical Bulletin 30(1).

Bindon, J.R. 1984. "The Body Build and Composition of Samoan Children: Relationships to Infant Feeding Patterns and Infant Weight-for-length Status", Journal Article, 63(4), Dept. of Anthropology, University of Alabama, Alabama, U.S.A.

Boultion, J.J.C., Roroley, M.P. 1979. "Nutritional Studies During Early Childhood: Incidental Observations of Temperament, Habits and Experiences of Ill-health", *Australian Paediatric Journal* 15(2).

Brock, J.F. and Austret, M. 1952, "Kwashiorkor in Africa", *World Health Organisation,* Geneva: Monograph Series, No. 8.

Brunn, S. 1986. "Grass Roots Support for Breast-feeding", *World Health Forum* 7(1).

Caldwell, J.C. 1979. "Education as a Factor in Mortality Decline: An Examination of Nigeria Data", *Population Studies 30.*

Capurro, M.T., Beas, F., and Schmidt, B.J. 1984. "Breast-feeding and Socio-economic Level of Chilean Infants Under 1 Year of Age", *Journal of Revista Children De Paediatria* 55(3).

Carvajal, J. , Rosero, L., and Sosa, D. 1979. "Evaluation of Family Planning Programme in Costa Rica", Department Publicatons, Director General De Estadisticay Censos, 1981.

Central Technical Committee on Health and Nutrition. 1990. *Monograph on Integrated Training on Nutritional Programmes for Mother and Child Development,* Department of Women and Child Development, Government of India, New Delhi.

Cleland, J., Ruststein, S. 1986. "Contraception and Birth Spacing", *International Family Planning Perspectives* 12(3).

Cochrane, S.H., O'Hara, D.J., and Leslie, J. 1980. *The Effect of Education on Health,* World Staff Working Paper No. 405, Washington, D.C.

Cooper, R.H. 1985. "Control of Acute Diarrhoeal Diseases in Children: A Document for Nurses, Social Workers, Teachers", *Programme of Development of Information on Early Childhood,* Technical Report, International Children's Centre, Paris, France.

Counsilman, J.J., Mackay, E.V. 1985. "Cigarette Smoking by Pregnant Women with Particular Reference to Their Past and Subsequent Breast-feeding Behaviour", *Australian and Newzeland Journal of Obstetrics and Gynaecology* 25(2).

Crawford, D. , and Worseley, A. 1984. "Vitamins, Health and Disease: Australians Perception of Vitamins, Minerals and Dietary Supplements", *Journal of Food and Nutrition* 41(4).

Dagan, R. , Sofu, S., Klish, W.J., et al. 1984. "Infant Feeding Practices among Bedovins in Transition from Semi-nomadic to Settlement Conditions in the Neger Area of Israel", *Journal of Medical Sciences* 20(11), November 1984, Israel.

Danforth, D.N. 1982. "Other Complications and Disorders Due to Pregnancy", *Obstetrics and Gynaecology* Ed. Danforth, D.N., Dignam, W.J., Handricks, C.H., and Maeck, J.V.S.4th Ed., Philadelphia: Harper and Row.

Datta Banik., N.D. "Some Observation on Feeding Programmes, Nutrition and Growth of Pre-school Children in an Urban Community", *Indian Journal of Paediatrics* 44(353).

Datta Banik, N.D., Krishna, R., Mane, S.I.S., and Tasker, A.D. 1970. "A Longitudinal Study of Physical Growth of Children from Birth Upto 5 Years of Age in Delhi," *Journal of Medical Research* (58).

Datta, M.S., Sharma, S.L., et al. 1984. "Feeding Practices of Infants and Children in Rural and Urban Areas of Himachal Pradesh", *Indian Paediatrics* 21(3).

Desweemer, C. , Kielmann, A.A., Parker, R.L. 1983. *Indicators of Nutritional Risk,* Monograph Chapter, World Bank Research Publication.

Devdas, R.P., Eswaran, P.P., and Ponnammal, K. 1977. "Diet and Nutrition in the First Year of Life. Part II Cross-sectional cum-

Semi Longitudinal Study of Physical Measurements," *Indian Journal of Nutrition and Dietetics* 14.

Dingle, J.H., Badger, G.F., and Jordon, W.S. 1964. "Common Respiratory Diseases: Incidence by Size of Family", *Illness in the Home: A Study of 25,000 Illnesses in a Group of Cleveland Families*, Cleveland, Ohio: Press of Western Reserve University.

Director of Census Operations, Andhra Pradesh. 1986. *District Census Hand Book, Chittoor,* Census of India, 1981, Series 2, Andhra Pradesh.

Donglass, J.W.B., and Blomfield, J.M. 1958. *Children Under Five,* London: George Alien & Uniwin Ltd.

Draper, N.R., and Smith, H. 1981: *Applied Regression Analysis,* New York: John Wiley & Sons.

D'Souza, Stan., and C. Cten. 1980. "Sex Differentials in Mortality in Rural Bangladesh," *Population and Development Review 6(2).*

Dunn, P.M. 1979. "Low-birth Weight, Incidence, Aetiology, and Prevention", *Maternity Services in the Developing World: What the Community Needs (Proceedings of the Seventh Study Group of the Royal College of Obstetricians and Gynaecologis,* Ed. Philpott, R.H. Sep. 1979.

Ebrahim, G.J. 1978. "Developing Countries", *Journal of National Institute of Health and Family Welfare,* New Delhi, India.

Elegbe, I. 1981. *Traditional Methods of Weaning: An Implication for Intensive Health Education* Monograph, Faculty of Health Sciences, University of Ife, Ile-Ife, Nigeria.

Erik Eckholm., and Frank Record. 1976. *Two Faces of Malnutrition,* World Watch Paper 9, World Watch Institute, Washington.

ESCAP. 1979. *Regional Workshop on Techniques of Analysis of World Fertility Survey Data,* Asian Population Studies Series, No. 44. 1981. *Multivariate Analysis of Nuptiality and Fertility for Selected ESCAP countries* Asian Population Studies Series, No. 59.

——*1984. Multivariate Analysis of Nuptiality and Fertility for Selected ESCAP Countries,* Asian Population Studies Series, No. 59.

——1985. *Multivariate Area Analysis of the Efficiency of the Family Planning Programme and It's Impact on Fertility Peninsular Malasia,* Asian Population Studies Series No. 66.

——1986. *Multivariate Area Analysis of the Efficiency of Family Planning Programme and It's Impact on Fertility in Bangladesh,* Asian Population Studies Series No. 67.

Fernandez, E.L., and Guthrie, G.M. 1984. "Belief Systems and Breast-feeding Among Filipino Urban Poor", *Journal of Social Sciences and Medicine* 19(9).

Forman, M.R. 1984. "Reivew of Research on the Factors Associated with Choice and Duration of Infant Feeding in Less-developed Countries", *Journal of Paediatrics* 74(4).

Frank, L. Mott. 1982. *Infant Mortality in Kenya: Evidence from the Kenya Fertility Survey,* W.F.S. Scientific Reports, No. 32, August, 1982. WFS, London.

Gandotra, M.M., Das, N., and Dey Devamani. 1982. 'Infant Mortality and Its Causes in Gujarat', Baroda Population Research Centre, Baroda, India.

Geissler, C., Galloway, D.H., and Margen, S. 1978 "Lactation and Pregnancy in Iran: Social and Economic Aspects", *American Journal of Clinical Nutrition* 31(1).

Ghai, O.P. 1985. *Understanding and Managing Acute Diarrhoea in Infants and Young Children,* All India Institute of Medical Sciences, New Delhi, India.

Ghosh, S. 1986. "Descrimination Begins at Birth", *Paediatrics* 23(1).

Goldenbug, P., Novo, N.F., Sigulem, D.M. 1984. "Assessment of Nutritional Condition and Duration of Breast-feeding", Revista De Saude Publicas 18(4).

Gomes, F., et al. 1956. Journal of Tropical Paediatrics 2.

Gopalan, G., and Vijayaraghavan, K. 1971. *Nutrition Atlas of India*, National Institute of Nutrition, Hyderabad, India.

Government of Andhra Pradesh. 1980. *Sixth Five Year Plan 1980-85, Andhra Pradesh* Draft. Vol. 1. Hyderabad, India.

Graham, G.G. 1968. *Calorie Deficiencies and Protein Deficiencies London; London Churchill.*

Grant, J.P. 1984. *The State of the World's Children* 1984. New York: United Nation's Children's Fund (UNICEF).

——1992. The State of the World's Children 1992. London: Oxford University Press.

Gunasekaran, S. 1988. "Correlates of Infant Mortality in Madurai District, Tamil Nadu", *Infant Mortality in India: Differentials and Determinants,* Ed. Anrudh, K. Jain., and Pravin Visaria. New Delhi: Sage Publication.

Gupta, S.B., Srinivasa, B.C., Vidya Bhushan., Sharma, P. 1984. "Impact of ICDS in Uttar Pradesh", *Indian Journal of Medical Research* 79.

Haager, J. 1985. "An Estimate of the Prevalence of Child Malnutrition in Developing Countries", *World Health Statistics Quarterly* 32(3).

Habitch J.P., Martorella, R., Yarbrough, E., Malia, R.M., Klein, R.E. 1974. "Height, Weight Standards for Pre-school Children: How Relevant are Ethnic Differences in Growth Potential?", *Lancet* 1.

Hambreaus, L. 1979. "Maternal Diet and Human Milk Composition", *Maternal Nutrition During Pregnancy and Lactation: A Nestle Foundation Workshop* Ed. Aebi, H., A and White Head, R. Switzerland: Luty Lansanne, (Nestle Foundation Publication Series No. 1).

Hamill, P.V.V. 1977. *NCHS Growth Curves for Children Birth—18 Years*. U.S., Department of Health, Education and Welfare.

Hanafy, M.M., Morsey, M.R.A., Seddick, Y., Habib, Y.A., and El Lozy, M. 1972. "National Nutritional and Lactation Performances: A Study in Urban Alexandria," *Journal of Tropical and Environmental Child Health* 18(3).

Harrison, U.A. 1979. "Approach to Reducing Maternal and Peri-natal Mortality in Africa," *Maternity Services in the Developing World: What the Community Needs; Proceedings of the Seventh Study Group of the Royal College of Obstetricians and Gynaecologists,* Ed. Philopott, R.H. Sept. 1979.

Hasan, J., Khan, Z., and Sinha, S.N. 1991. "Socio-cultural Factors Influencing Nutritional Status of Infants—A Longitudinal Study", *Indian Journal of Maternal and Child Health* 2(3).

Hay, S. 1971. "Incidence of Selected Congenital Malformation in Lowa, " *American Journal of Epidemiology 94(6)*.

Holla, M. 1985. "Vital Statistics System—A Major Source of Information on Infant and Child Mortality." , *Indian Journal of Paediatrics 52.*

Hook, E.B. 1976. "Estimates of Maternal Age Specific Issues of" a Down - Syndrome Birth in Women Aged 34-41", *Lancet* ii.

—— and Fasia, I.J. 1978. "Frequency of Down Syndrome in Live Births by Single Year Maternal Age Interval of a Massachusetts Study", *Teratology* 17(3), June 1978.

Horger, E.O., and Smythe, A.R. 1977. "Second Pregnancy in Women Over Forty", *Obstetrics and Gynaecology* 49(3).

Huffman, S.L. 1984. "Determinants of Breast-feeding in Developing Countries: An Overview and Policy Implications", *Journal of Studies in Family Planning* 15(4), July-Aug. 1984.

ICMR. 1972. *Growth and Physical Development of Indian Children* ICMR Technical Report Series No. 18.

——*1984. Studies on Weaning and Supplementary Foods,* ICMR Technical Report Series No. 27.

Idris, I.S. 1984. "Nutritional Status of Infants and Children, 0-3 Years in Southern District of Shendi Region (Nile Province)", Thesis Submitted for Partial Fulfilment of Master of Community Medicine, University of Khartoum, Sudan.

IIPS. 1986. "Baseline Survey on Fertility, Mortality and Related Factors in Maharashtra: Summary of the Findings and Programme Implications", *IIPS, News Letter* 27(2).

Indian Academy of Paediatrics. 1984. "Recommendations on Breast-feeding: Policy Statement Based on Report of Special Committee, 1983," *Indian Paediatrics* 21(1).

Indira Bai, K. , Raghavaprasad, K., Srinath, V., Ravikumaran., Obul Reddy, C. 1979. "Nutritional and Anthropometric Profile of Primary School Children in Rural Andhra Pradesh", *Indian Paediatrics* 16(12).

Indira Bai, K. , Sastry, V.N., Obul Reddy, C. 1981. "A Comparative Study of Feeding Pattern of Infants in Rural and Urban Areas", *Indian Journal of Paediatrics* 48(392).

Indira Kapoor. 1979. "Childhood: It's Developmental Aspects," *The Journal of Family Welfare* XXVI. No. 2. Dec. '79.

International Nutrition Communication Service (INCS). 1982. *Maternal and Infant Nutrition Reviews, Ecuador: Guide to Literature,* Monograph. Nutrition Mass Education Development Centre, INCS, 1982, United States.

——1983. *Maternal and Infant Nutrition Reviews, Burma;*

Guide to Literature Monograph. Nutrition Mass Education Development Centre, INCS, 1983, United States.

——1983. *Maternal and Infant Nutrition Reviews, Bolivia: Guide to Literature,* Monograph. Nutrition Mass Education Development Centre, INCS, 1983, United States.

——1983. *Maternal and Infant Nutrition Reviews, Mali: Guide to Literature,* Monograph. Nutrition Mass Education Department Centre, INCS, 1984, United States.

——1984 *Maternal and Infant Nutrition Reviews, Indonesia: Guide to Literature,* Monograph. Nutrition Mass Education Department Centre, INCS, 1983 United States.

Jelliffe, D.B. 1966. "The Assessment of the Nutritional Status of the Community", *World Health Organisation* Geneva: Monograph Series, No. 53.

John, A. Ross., Marjorie Rich Janet., Molzan., Michael Pensak. 1988. *Family Planning and Child Survival in 100 Developing Countries* Centre for Population and Family Health, Columbia University, Columbia.

John B. Wyon., and John E. Gordon. 1971. *The Khanna Study: Population Problems in Rural Punjab* Cambridge: Harward University Press.

John Cleland and Jerome Ginneken. 1989. "Maternal Schooling and Childhood Mortality", *Health Interventions and Mortality Change in Developing Countries*, Ed. Allan G. Hill., and Roberts, D.F. Journal of Bio-social Science Supplement, No.10. Parks Foundation, Cambridge, England.

John Knodell., and Nibhon Debavalya. 1980, *Trends and Differentials in Breast-feeding in Thailand* Institute of Population, Bangkok, Thailand.

Jones,, D.A. 1986. "Attitudes of Breast-feeding Mothers: A Survey of 649 Mothers," *Journal of Social Sciences and Medicine* 23(11).

Jorapur, P.B. 1979. *Health, Nutrition and Family Planning in Karnataka,* Population Study Centre, S.V.University, Tirupati.

Kanitkar Tara., and Murthy, B.N. 1989. "Factors Associated in Rajasthan and Orissa", *Infant Mortality in India: Differentials and Determinants*, Ed. Anrudh, K. Jain., and Pravin Visaria. New Delhi: Sage Publications.

Kaur, S., Puri, R., Bajaj, S. 1983. "Feeding Practices, Among Children of Different Castes in Rural Ludiana", *Indian Journal of Paediatrics,* Home Science, Punjab Agricultural University, Ludhiana, India.

Keller, N. , and Fillmore, C.M. 1983. "Prevalence of Protein-energy Malnutrition," *World Health Statistics Quarterly* 36(2).

Kesasree, N., et al. 1982. "Feeding Pattern of Infants in Davanagere", *Indian Journal of Paediatrics* 49.

Khan, M.E. 1988. "Infant Mortality in Uttar Pradesh: A Micro-level Study", *Infant Mortality in India: Differentials and Determinants* Ed. Anrudh, K.Jain., and Pravin Visaria. New Delhi: Sage Publications.

Khan, M.E., Ghosh, S.K., Dastidar and Ratnajeet Singh. 1986. "Nutrition and Health Practices Among Rural Women—A Case Study of Uttar Pradesh, India", *Journal of Family Welfare* 31(1).

Khan, M.E. 1991. "Family Planning in Primary Health Care", *Journal of the Council for Social Development* 21(1).

Khan, M.U. 1981. "Victims of Childhood Deaths", *Indian Journal of Paediatrics 48.*

——1984.. "Breast-feeding, Growth and Diarrhoea in Rural Bangladesh Children", *Human Nutrition; Clinical Nutrition* 38, (2) ICDDRE, Dhaka-12, Bangladesh.

Khanjanasthaiti, P., Supachaturan, P., Mekananda, P., Srimusikapodh, V., Choopauya, K., and Leesuwan, V. 1973. "Growth of Infants and Pre-school Children," *Journal of Medical Association of Thailand* (56).

Kielmann, A.A., De Sweemer, et al. 1983. *Analysis of Morbidity and Mortality,* A World Bank Research Publication Monograph, Maryland: John Hopkins University Press, Baltimore.

Kings, F.S 1984. "The First Weeks of Breast-feeding," *IPPF Medical-Bulletin* 18(5).

Kown, E.H., Kim, T.R., Hong, I.W., AHN, Y.O. and Kim E.I. 1975. "The Interrelationship Between Family Planning and Child Health", *Social Journal of Medicine* 16(4).

Krishnamurthy, S. 1970. "Amenorrhoea in Relation to Age, Parity and Breast-feeding", *Bulletin of the Gandhigram Institute of Rural Health and Family Planning* (1) July 1970.

Kumari, S., Jain P., Arora, U., Pruthi, R.K. 1982. "Growth of Breast-fed infants: A Longitudinal Study", Indian *Journal of Paediatrics* 49(12).

Kumari, S., Pruthi, P.K., Mehra R., and Sehgal, S. 1985. "Breast-feeding: Physical Growth During Infancy", *Indian Journal of Paediatrics* 52.

Kumar, V., Sharma, ., Khanna, P., Vanaza, K. 1981. "The Growth of Breast-fed *vs* Bottle Feeding—Impact on Growth in Urban Infants", *Indian Journal of Paediatrics*, 49.

Lakshmamma, T. 1991. *Pregnancy and Responsible Parenthood,* New Delhi: Discovery Publishing House.

Lakshmamma, T., Prabhakara Reddy, B. and Subramanyam, G. 1991. "Health and Feeding Practices of Children in Andhra Pradesh", *Journal of Gandhi Medical College, Hyderabad* 3(5).

Leela Visaria. 1988. "Levels, Trends and Determinants of Infant Mortality in India", *Infant Mortality in India: Differentials and Determinants,* Ed. Anrudha, K. Jain., and Pravin Visaria. New Delhi: Sage Publications.

Leela Raman., Vasanthi, G., Parvathi, C., Vasumathi, N., Rawal, A., Visveswar Rao, K., and Balakrishnan, N. 1989. "Growth and Development of Infants in Urban Slums of Hyderabad," *The Indian Journal of Nutrition and Dietetics* (26) .

Lucia De Freitas, C., Romani, S., Emigo, H. 1986. "Breast-feeding and Malnutrition in Rural Areas of North East-Brazil" , *Bulletin of the PAN American Health Organisation* 20(2).

Luwang, N.C., and Gupta, V.M. 1980. "Anaemia in Pregnancy in a Rural Community Influence of Dietary Intake in the Multifactorial Actiology", *The Indian Journal of Nutrition and Dietetics* (17).

Madhu Nath, and Girvani, P. 1979. "Diet and Nutrition of Pregnant and Lactating Women and Infants of Urban Slums of Hyderabad", *Indian Journal of Nutrition and Dietetics* (16).

Mahapatra, S.S. 1984. "Study of Peri-natal Mortality and Related Factors in Lanjigarh, A Tribal ICDS Block", *Indian Paediatrics* 21(8).

Mahendale, S.M., Karanadikar, V.N., Natu, N.N. 1985. "Some Aspects of Evaluation of Pune Urban ICDS Project", *Medical Journal of Western India*. 13.

Margaret Comeron and Yugue Hazavander. 1983. *Manual on Feeding of Infants and Young Children:* New Delhi: Oxford Press.

Mata, L. 1985. *The Fight Against Diarrhoeal Diseases: The Case of Costa Rica,* Monograph Chapter, Liege, Belgium.

McLaren, D.S. et al. 1967. "A Simple Scoring System for Classifying the Severe Forms of Protein - Calorie Malnutrition of Early Childhood", *Lancet* i.

Meera Cheterjee. 1985. "Health for All: Whither the Child?", *Social Action* 35(3).

Meyer, M.B. 1978. "How Does Maternal Smoking Affect Birth Weight and Maternal Weight Gain? Evidence from the Ontario Peri-natal Mortality Study", *American Journal of Obstetrics and Gyneocology* 131(8).

Miller, B.B. 1981. *The Enlarged Sex: Neglect of Female Children in Rural North India* Ithca.

Ministry of Home Affairs. 1983. *Survey of Infant and Child Mortality 1979* New Delhi: Government of India.

Muftu, Y. 1981. "Patterns of Child Morbidity and Mortality in Developing Countries, with a Special Reference to Turkey", *The Turkish National Paediatrics Society* 3(2).

Mukerjee, D.K. 1979. "Longitudinal Study of the Pattern of Illness in Under Previledged Bengali Hindu Children from Birth Upto 18 Months of Age,", *Indian Journal of Public Health,* 23, No. 1.

National Centre for Health Statistics, 1973. "A Study of Infant Mortality from Linked Records by Age of Mother, Total Birth Order, and Other Variables: United States, 1960 Low-birth Cohort". Washington, DC, US 'Department of Health, Education and Welfare (Vital and Health Statistics, Series 20, No. 14).

Nations', M. 1983. "Spirit Possession to Enteric Pathogens, the Role of Traditional Healing in Diarrhoeal Disease Control", *Monograph Chapter International Conference on Oral Rehydration Theraphy Proceedings,* Monograph Chapter. Agency for International Development, AID., Bureau for Science and Technology, Washington., D.C.

Nortzon F. 1984.. "Trends in Infant Feeding in Developing Countries", *Journal of Paediatrics* 74.

Ogbeide, 0., Osuhor, P.C. 1984. "Morbidity and Mortality Patterns Among Malnourished Children in Benin City, Nigeria", *Tropical Doctor* 14(4). Dept. of Community Health, College of Medical Sciences, University *of* Benia, Benin City, Nigeria.

O'Malley, L.S.S. (ed). 1968. *Modern Indian and the West,* London: Oxford University Press.

Omran, A.R., and Standly, C.C. (ed). 1976. *Family Formation Patterns and Health—An International Collaborative Study in India, Iran, Lebanon, Phillippine, and Turkey,* Geneva: WHO.

Opena, M. , Ramos., L. Ramoso. , T., Inciong. 1977. "Dietary Survey Among Pregnant and Lactating Women in a Resettlement: Dietary Practices and Beliefs", *Phillippine Journal of Nutrition* 30(3).

Pan American Health Organisation (PAHO). 1969. *Maternal Nutrition and Family Planning with American Report of a PAHO Technical Group Meeting,* Washington, Scientific Publication No. 201.

Parker, R.L., Labbok, M.H., et al. 1986. Primary Health Care and Family Planning Operations Research in Church Sponsored Community Programmes in Kenya, Unpublished Work, USAID Contract No. AID/DSPE-Coo55, United States.

Pascoe, J.M., Bergu, A. 1985. "Attitude of High School Girls in Israel and the United States Towards Breast-feeding", *Journal of Adolescent Health Care* 6(1).

Patodi, R.K., Tiwari, S.C., Mathur, L.K. 1976. "Infant Feeding Practices in Urban and Rural Area in Madhya Pradesh", *Indian Journal of Paediatrics 43.*

Pelto, G.H., Lunglaho, M.S. 1984. "The Weaning Process", *Journal of World Health,* October 1984.

Petro-Barvazian, *A.,* and Behai, M. 1978. "Problem Identification: Low Birth Weight—A Major Global Problems", *Birth Weight Distribution—An Indication of Social Development* Ed. Sterky, G., and Mallanadu, L. Geneva. Swedish Agency for Research Corporation with Developing Countries and World Health Organisation, (SAKE Report No. R. 2, 1978).

Pisharoti, K.A., and Gunasekaran, S. 1976. "Family Formation and Childhood Mortality", eds. Omran, A.R., and Stanley, C.C. *Family Formation Patterns and Health* World Health Organisation, Geneva.

Popkin, B., Hamilton, S., and Sicer, D. 1984. *Women and Nutrition in Low-Income Countries*, South Hadley, Massachusetts, Bergin & Canvey.

Poplhin, B.M. 1976. "Nutrition and Labour Productivity", *Social Science and Medicine* 12(3-4C).

——1980. "Time Allocation of the Mother and Child Nutrition", *Ecology of Food and Nutrition* 9(7).

Population Reports. 1979. *Age at Marriage and Fertility* Series M. Number 4, Population Information Programme, The John Hopkins University, U.S.A.

——1981. *Benefits of Breast-feeding Series;* J. Number 24, Population Information Programme, Johon Hopkins University, U.S.A.

——1984. *Healthier Mothers and Children Through Family Planning,* Series J. No. 27, Population Information Programme, John Hopkins University, U.S.A.

Prentice, A.M., Whitehead, R.G., Watkinson, M., Land, W.H., and Cole T.J. 1983. "Pre-natal Dietary Supplementation of African Women and Birth-weight", *Lancet* i.

Protein Foods and Nutrition Development Association of India (PFNDAOI). 1973. *Better Foods for Better Nutrition: Report of the Hyderabad Workshop Based on a Food Habit Survey to South India,* Bombay, India.

Puffer, R.R., and Rao C.V. 1975. *Birth Weight, Maternal Age, and Birth Orders: Three Important Determinants of Infant Mortality* Scientific Publication No. 294, Pan American Health Organisation, Washington.

Rajalakshmi, R. 1979. "Gestation and Lactation Performance in Relation to the Plane of Maternal Nutrition," *Maternal Nutrition During Pregnancy and Lactation: A Nestle Foundation Workshop* ed. Aebi, H., and Whitehead, R. Switzerland: Nestle Foundation Publication Series, No. 1.

Rajammal, P., Devadas., Parvathi, P., Easwaran, and Ponnammal, K. 1977. "Diet and Nutrition in the First Year of Life: Part-II Cross Sectional-cum Semi-Longitudinal Study of Physical Measurements", *Indian Journal of Nutritional Dietetics* 14.

Rajimol Cherian., Rajeshree, S., Soman, C.R. 1988. "Anthropometric Assessment of Malnutrition Comparison of Two Age Independent Criteria", *The Indian Journal of Nutrition and Dietetics* (25).

Ramadasmurthy, V., and Moharan, M. 1984. *Your Health and Nutrition,* National Institute of Nutrition, Indian Council of Medical Research, Hyderabad, India.

Rao, K.V., Ram, P. 1982. "Appropriate Age for Introduction of Supplementary Foods for Infants: A Statistical Appraisal", *Nutrition,* 32(4/5/6), National Institute of Nutrition, Hyderabad, India.

Rayappa, P. Hanumantha., Samuel, M. Johnson. 1989. "Universal Immunisation Programme: An Evaluation Study in Hassan District," *Annual Report* 88-89. Population Research Centre, Institute of Social and Economic Change, Bangalore.

Reddy, P.H. 1989. "Utilisation of M.C.H. and Family Welfare Services in Andhra Pradesh", *Health and Family Welfare Services in India,* Ed. Basantibala Jeena, and Rabindranath Pati. New Delhi: Ashish Publishing House.

Registrar General of India. 1983. *Social and Cultural Tables,* Census of India, 1981 (based on 20 per cent sample data), Ministry of Home Affairs, New Delhi.

——1988. *Sample Registration Bulletin* XXII (i) Ministry of Home Affairs, New Delhi.

Registrar General of India. 1990. *Survey of Cause of Death (Rural)* Annual Report, 1988. Series 3, No.21. Office of the Registrar General, India, Ministry of Home Affairs.

——1991. *Sample Registration Bulletin* XXV (i), Ministry of Home Affairs, New Delhi.

——1991. *Registrar General's News Letter,* Vol 22, No.3. Office of Registrar General, India, Ministry of Home Affairs.

Roman, E., Doyle, P., Berai, V., Alberman, F., and Pharoah, P. 1978. "Foetal Loss, Gravidity and Pregnancy Order," *Early Human Development* 2(2), July 1978.

Rowland, M.G. 1983. *Epidemiology of Childhood Diarrhoea in the Gambia,* Monograph Chapter, Plenum Press, New York, U.S.A.

Rueda, R. 1980. The Nutritional Component in the Integrated Mother-Child Health Programmes, The Japanese Organisation for International Cooperation in Family Planning (JOICEP) and Association, First American Conference on Integreated Programmes, Tokyo.

Rutstein Shea Oscer. 1983. *Infant and Child Mortality: Levels, Trends and Demographic Differentials,* Comparative Studies, Cross-National Summaries, No. 24, Sep. 83. World Fertility Survey, London.

Sabis, N.I., Ebrahim, G.J. 1934. "Are Daughters More at Risk Than Sons in Some Societies". *Journal of Tropical Paediatrics* 30(4). Tropical Child Health Unit, Institute of Child Health, London.

Saeed Qureshi, M. and Omran, A.R. 1981. 'Palustan', *Family Formation Patterns and Health: Further Studies*, Ed. Omran, A.R., Standley, C.C., Ochoa, G., Gil, A., Hamman, H., Sherbini, F. , El., Raza, B., Khan, T., Bonstani, F. EL., Geneva: W.H.O.

Saksena, D.N., and Srivastava, J.N. 1980. *Child Mortality and Family Formation Patterns in Lucknow City,* Population Research Centre, Department of Economics, Lucknow University, Lucknow. (memeographed).

Satapathy, R.K., Sarangi, B. , Das, O.K. 1984. "A Community Survey of Infant Feeding Practices in Berhampur , South Orissa", *Indian Paediatrics* 21(3).

Schmodit, B.J. 1983. "Breast-feeding and Infant Morbidity and Mortality in Developing Countries", *Journal of Paediatric Gastroenterology and Nutrition* Discipline of Puericulture and Social Paediatrics, Department of Paediatrics, Brazil.

Senapati, S.K., Bhattacharya, S., and Das, O.K. 1990. "The Girl Child: An Exposition of Their Status", *Indian Journal of Community Medicine,* Jan-March, XV(i).

Sengupta, S.K. 1971. "Demographic Indices of Mortality in Relation to Public Health", *Report of the Workshop on Public Health,* Population Council of India, New Delhi.

Sewaed, J.F., Serdula, M.K., 1984. "Infant Feeding and Infant Growth", *Concet.*

Shakir, A., et al. 1972. "Pattern of Protein-calorie Malnutrition in Young Children Attending an Out Patient Clinic in Baghdad", *Lancet* ii.

Shanghai Child Health Care Coordinating Group. 1974. "Growth and Development of Shanghai Infants", *Chinese Medical Journal* 10.

Simpson, S.P. 1984. "Causal Analysis of Infant Deaths in Hawaii", *American Journal of Epidemiology* 119 (6).

Siqueira, A.A.P. DE., Santhosh, J.L.F., Saqueto, C.G., Luz, E.T., Aracico, M.C.A. D. 1985. "Effects of Maternal Nutritional State and Smoking Habits on Intrauterine and Pre-natal Growth", *Revista de Saude Publica* 19(1).

Srinivasan, K., Kartikan, T., Ahmed, V., and Sarangi, L. 1985. *Report on the Base Line Survey on Fertility, Mortality and Related Factors in Orissa,* International Institute for Population Studies, Bombay, India.

Stauart, H.C. and Stevenson, S.S. 1959. "Physical Growth and Development", *Text Book of Paediatrics* ed. Nelson, W. 7th ed. Philadelphia, Saundus, 1959.

Subramanyam, G., et al. 1985 'Mortality Pattern Among Children (0-3) Years in the Slum Areas of Vijayawada, Siddhartha Medical Journal 2(4).

Sunderlal. 1980. "Better Primary Health Care Services Utilisation Through Integrated Child Development Services Scheme in Haryana", *Indian Journal of Paediatrics* 47(387).

——1985. "Early Childhood Mortality in an ICDS Block, Haryana", *Indian Journal of Community Medicine* 10(1).

Swensan, I. 1977. "Expected Reduction in Foetal and Infant Mortality by Prolonged Pregnancy Spacing in Rural Bangladesh", *Bangladesh Development Studies,* 5(1).

Talwar, Prem, P. 1988. "Infant Mortality, Some Evidence from Rural Madhya Pradesh", *Infant Mortality in India: 3 Differentials and Determinants,* Ed. Anrudh, K. Jain., and Pravin Visaria. New Delhi: Sage Publications.

Tanner, J.M., White House, R.P.I., Takaishi, M. 1965. Standards from Birth to Maturity for Height, Weight, and Weight Velocity: British Children, *Arch Dis Child* 1966. 41.

Trowell, H.C. 1941. "Infantile Pellagra", *Transactions of the Royal Society of Tropical Medicine and Hygiene* 33.

Trussel, J. and Hammerslough, C. 1983. "A Hazards Model Analysis of the Covariates of Infant and Child Mortality in Srilanka", *Demography* 20(1).

Tyagi, B.N. 1983. "A Review of Diarrhoeal Disease Control Programme in India", *Health and Population Perspectives and Issues* 9(4).

U.N. 1981. *Population Research Leeds: Significance of the Relationship Between Nutrition and Human Reproduction* No. 8 ESCAP, Bangkok.

U.N. 1985. *Socio-economic Differentials in Child Mortality in Developing Countries,* Dept. of Social and Economic Affairs, U.N. New York.

U.N. 1988. *Mortality of Children Under Age 5, World Estimates and Projections,* New York.

UNESCO. 1975. *Population Education in Asia, a Source Book of Population: Quality of Life Themes,* Regional Office for Education in Asia, Bangkok.

United Nations Food and Agricultural Organisation (FAO). 1973. *Energy and Protein Requirements,* Nutrition Meetings Report Series No. 52.

UNICEF. 1985: *The State of the World's Children,* New York: UNICEF.

——1987. The State of the World's Children, New York: UNICEF.

Urmila Sharma, 1987. "Utilising Dais of Impart Health and Nutrition Education: Impact on Growth", *Indian Journal of Paediatrics* (54).

Van Ginnehen, J.K., Kok. P.W. 1934. *Summary of Findings and Implications for Public Health* Monograph Chapter. Medical Research Centre, Nairobi, Kenya.

Van Weiringer, J.C. 1972. *Seculiar Changes of Growth: 1964-1966, Height and Weight Surveys in the Netherlands in Historical*

Prospective Leider: Netherlands Institute for Preventive Medicine.

Vega-Franco, L., Alanis, S.E., et al. 1984. "Influence of Breast-feeding and Weaning on the Nutritional Status of Infants", *Boletin Medico Del Hospital Infantil Do Mexico* 41(11).

Venkataramani. 1986. "Born to Die", *India Today,* June 15, 1986.

Vijayaraghavan, K., and Rao Parvati. 1973. "Food Habits and Attitudes in Some Parts of Andhra Pradesh", *Better Foods for Better Nutrition: Report of the Hyderabad Workshop Based on a Food Habit Survey in South India*, Nutrition Development Association of India, (PFNDAI), Bombay, India.

Vijayaraghavan, K., Singh, D. Swaminathan, M.C. 1971. "Height and Weight of Well Nourished Indian School Children", *Indian Journal of Medical Research* 59.

Visweswara Rao, K., and Gopalan, C. 1971. "Family Size and Nutritional Status", *Report of the Workshop on Family Health,* Population Council of India, New Delhi.

Vittchi, F.E. 1969. "Consideration on the Effect of Nutrition on the Body Composition and Physical Working Capacity of Young Gautamala Adults", *Amino Acid Fortification of Protein Foods,* Ed. Scimshaw, N.S., and Aftschul, A.M. MIT Press, Cambridge: MIT Press.

Waterlow, J.C. 1948. *Fatty Liver Disease in Infants in the British West Indies,* Research Council Special Report Series No. 263, H.M. Stationary Office, London.

Waterlow, J.C., Thomson, A.M. 1979, "Observation on the Adequacy of Breast-feeding", *Lancet* ii.

Waterstor, T. 1984. "Infants in Juba and Letters", *Lancet* ii.

Whichelow, M.J. 1975. "Calorie Requirements for. Successful Breast-feeding", *Archives of Diseases in Childhood* 50(8).

Whichelow, M.J. 1976. *Success and Failure of Breast-feeding in Relation to Energy Intake,* Proceedings of the Nutrition Society 35(2), 62A, 63A.

Whitehead, R.G. 1981. *Maternal Diet, Breast-feeding Capacity and Lactational Infertility:* Report of a UNU/WHO/IPPF/ Workshop held in Cambridge, United Kingdom, March 1981.

W.H.O. 1973. *Energy and Protein Requirements,* WHO Technical Report Series No. 522.

——1979. *Measurement of Nutritional Impact: A Guidelines for the Measurement of the Nutritional Impact of the Supplementary Feeding Programmes Aimed at Vulnerable Groups* WHO/FAO/79.1.

——1981. *Contemporary Pattern of Breast-feeding* Report on the World Health Organisation Collaboration Study on Breast-feeding, W.H.O. Geneva.

——1983. *Infant and Child Mortality in the Third World,* W.H.O. Geneva.

Williams, C.D., and Jelliffe, D.B. 1976. *Mother and Child Health,* London: The English Language Book Society and Oxford Unviersity Press.

Wincoff, B. and Brown, G. 1980. "Nutrition, Population and Health: Theoretical and Practical Issues", *Social Science and Medicine* 14 C(2).

Winilheff Beverly. 1983 "The Effects of Birth Spacing on Child and Maternal Health", *Studies in Family Planning* 14(10).

Wolfers, David., and Scrimshaw, Susan. 1975. "Child Survival and Interval Between Pregnancies in Ecuador", *Population Studies* 29(2).

Woodbury, R.M. 1925. *Causal Factors in Infant Mortlity: a Statistical Study Based on Investigations in Eight Cities,* Monograph, Children's Bureau Publication No. 142, Government Printing Office, Washington.

Wray, J.D. 1978. Maternal Nutrition, Breast-feeding and Infant Survival. *Nutrition and Human Reproduction,* ed. Mosley, W.H.O. Supported and Organised by the National Institute of Child Health and Human Development, Held at National Institute of Health, Bethesda, Maryland, Feb. 14-16, 1977, New York.

Wyon, Jhon, B., and Garden, John E. 1971. "A Long Term Perspective Type Field Study of Population Dynamics in Punjab, India", *Research in Family Planning* ed. Kisser. Princeton: Princeton University Press.

Yerushalmy, J., Bierman, J.M., Kempt, D.H., Conor, A., and French, F.E. 1956. "Longitudinal Studies of Pregnancy on the Island of Kausai, Territory of Hawaii: Analysis of Previous Reproductive History", *Journal of Obstetrics and Gynaecology* 71(1).

Yong, S., and Davidlf, N.B. 1985. "Trends and Levels of Mortality in China," *International Symposium on China's One-per Thousand Population Sampling Survey,* China Population Information Centre, Beejing.

Index

E

F

H

I

J

K

M

□□□